Malone House, Barnett Demesne, Malone Road, Belfast, BT9 5PB

Facilitated by: **Brian Garrett** (Solicitor)

Legacy
Legislation
Conference

SATURDAY
3 MARCH 2018

REGISTRATION
10 a.m. to 10.30 a.m.
Tea, Coffee and Scones

WELCOME AND INTRODUCTION
10.30 a.m. to 10.40 a.m.
Councillor **Jeffrey Dudgeon**, MBE

THE LEGACY BILL AND THE PROPOSED BODIES
10.40 a.m. to 12.30 p.m.

- **Neil Faris** (Solicitor) *Misconceptions on "Truth & Justice" – an Overview*
- Dr. **William Matchett** (Author)
- Dr. **Cillian McGrattan** (Ulster University) *"The possibilities are endless": Republican strategy and transitional justice*
- Dr. **Andrew Charles** (Community and voluntary sector) *The Past Being the Future*

A panel discussion will take place at the end of the morning session.

LUNCH
12.30 p.m. to 1.30 p.m.

LITIGATION CONTROVERSIES AND CONCLUSIONS
1.30 p.m. to 3.30 p.m.

- Dr. **Austen Morgan** (Barrister and historian) *The Past: Drawing a Line?*
- **Ken Funston** (South East Fermanagh Foundation Advocacy Manager) *The Victim's Perspective*
- **Trevor Ringland** (Solicitor/One Small Step) *Dealing with the Past – Properly or Not At All*
- **Danny Kinahan** (former MP for South Antrim) *Getting the Legislation Right*
- **Ben Lowry** (Deputy Editor of the Belfast News Letter)

There will be a panel discussion at the end of the afternoon session.

LEGACY

What to do about the Past in Northern Ireland?

Editor for the Malone House Group
Jeffrey Dudgeon

BELFAST PRESS

First published in April 2018 by Belfast Press

The authors © 2018

ISBN 978-1987449808

jeffreydudgeon@hotmail.com

Tel 079 2125 1874

Designed and typeset by Books Ulster/Library Ireland Media

www.booksulster.com

www.libraryireland.com

Cover photograph of the aftermath of the Enniskillen bomb in 1987 courtesy of Raymond Humphreys, Enniskillen

Foreword

This collection of papers stems from a conference on 3 March 2018 in Belfast's Malone House. The range of legal, academic and political speakers was impressive, more so because it is rarely heard. It is not the predominant voice in the media and certainly not the Academy or the funded sectors. Until the (initial) Loughinisland judgement earlier this year, in a judicial review brought by retired police officers, it was never heard in the courts. And those courts, our Supreme Court and the European Court of Human Rights (ECHR) are awash with Legacy cases and inquests.

We aimed to change that at Malone House by developing a new consensus on alternate ways to address the Past, ones that can bring peace of mind to innocent victims and justice – so far as that is possible.

By publishing our papers we are attempting to reshape the agenda and indeed the direction of travel. We hope to see this book read and seen far and wide but most especially in government, law schools and at Westminster where these matters are again being decided.

The long-promised Legacy Bill remains unpublished at the time of writing. Its proposed Haass-type bodies like HIU are deeply flawed and mindlessly complex. Indeed the Bill may never see the light of day. Indeed this we believe would be preferable with the issues approached in different, simpler and better ways.

The collapse of the NI Assembly and the fact that it had ceased to be a legislative body anyway, expatriating controversial law making – as with Legacy – to London means our perspective and actions have to refocus.

The view that the investigations of the Past can be time-limited by Parliament to five years is entirely misplaced. One opinion expressed from the floor at Malone House was that they would take 500 years. Given the refusal by the Foreign Office, and the Government generally, to argue otherwise, the dogma of ECHR Article 2 compliance on adequate investigations, goes unchallenged. The courts have no back stop and that version of Article 2 will remain supreme.

If left alone, it certainly means decades of litigation, as every inquest can be re-opened and probably will. And then re-opened again, alongside every 'concluded' HET case. (HET was actually a Strasbourg compromise. They can happen.) Otherwise, the shadow of the past can never be lifted.

The past will be our future and history will be rewritten.

My thanks, over and above those to the contributors, go to Nigel Macauley and Richard Kennedy for arrangements at Malone House and to Derek Rowlinson of Library Ireland Media for this book's typesetting and speedy production.

Jeffrey Dudgeon

24 March 2018

Event gave platform to key minority voices on legacy

5b|18   NL

A seminar on Saturday in Belfast examined the coming legacy legislation that will govern Northern Ireland's approach to the past.

It was a rare event, because scrutiny of legacy structures has overwhelmingly been from an angle that is positive to the 2014 Stormont House proposals.

A range of pressure groups, human rights lawyers, and politicians have agreed that that is the best way forward.

But some people who work with victims of the IRA, such as Kenny Donaldson and Ken Funston (whose brother was murdered by terrorists near the border), have been deeply concerned about the Stormont House structures.

They fear the proposals will not bring justice to IRA victims, and will concentrate on claims against the security forces. London is alert to these concerns and is trying to ensure the mooted Historical Investigations Unit (HIU) does not end up focusing to a disproportionate extent on state violence.

It is reassuring that the government is sensitive to these fears but disturbing that such an imbalance is impossible. Mr Funston and Mr Donaldson were among the people who contributed to Saturday's event, as did lawyers who have queried the structures, including Neil Faris and Austen Morgan.

One of the most powerful interventions of the day came from the floor, when Anne Graham, sister of the murdered lawyer Edgar, shot at point blank range on the verge of Queen's University in 1983, relayed her deep dissatisfaction with the Historical Enquiries Team's (HET) handling of her brother's case. The HIU will replace the HET.

The seminar was set up by Jeff Dudgeon, the Ulster Unionist councillor and former member of the party's team in the Haass talks. He is highly critical of the legacy structures.

These vital voices have not received anything like the coverage they deserve on legacy, as aggressive pro republican factions make the most noise. But London seems determined to implement Stormont House, so critics will have to engage fully with the consultation process.

Belfast News Letter, Morning View, 5 March 2018

Preface

Brian Garrett LL.B, FCI Arb, Solicitor

At the invitation of Jeffrey Dudgeon (Ulster Unionist Councillor, Belfast) who organised the event I was designated 'Facilitator' (i.e. Chair) at the Legacy Legislation Conference held at Malone House, Belfast, on Saturday 3 March 2018. I did not expect my role would prove difficult; I was wrong – not due to an unruly audience but rather because so many present had so much to say and were anxious to highlight their concerns. The event was clearly timely.

This booklet contains papers delivered by a range of the principal speakers. A wide spectrum of analysis and emphasis is covered, ranging from the detailed outline by Neil Faris of concern over the proposed legislation in terms of basic rights, to proposals by Trevor Ringland to meet the needs of 'The Past', critiques of Sinn Fein strategy (Dr. Austen Morgan, Dr. Andrew Charles and Dr. Cillian McGrattan), the role of the Westminster Parliament (Danny Kinahan), and the mounting concerns of innocent victims (Ken Funston, South East Fermanagh Foundation). The event ended with a powerful (and defiant) contribution by Ben Lowry (Deputy Editor, *The News Letter*) exposing the deceit underlying much of Sinn Fein propaganda when responding to events involving the security forces.

The Stormont House Agreement, concluded in December 2014, under the aegis (and participation) of both the UK and Irish Governments, proclaimed (Para 21);—

"As part of the transition to long-term peace and stability the participants agree that an approach to dealing with the past is necessary which reflects the following principles:—

- *Promoting reconciliation*
- *Upholding the rule of law*
- *Acknowledging and addressing the suffering of victims and survivors*
- *Facilitating the pursuance of justice and information recovery;*
- *Is human rights compliant*
- *Is balanced, proportionate, transparent, fair and equitable. "*

There followed proposals for some four new institutions (see Neil Faris paper). Now, more than three years later, none of these have been created and become operative; the Stormont Assembly has collapsed, concerns over failure to conduct inquests (in some cases dating back more than 30 years) and the Sinn Fein hypocritical indulgence in the language of human rights (with repeated references in their campaign calling for 'Equality and Respect') – all testify to both the political impasse and, worse, manifest inter-community distrust.

A recurring feature of the Legacy Conference was concern that human rights and justice issues were being hijacked for unscrupulous ends by Sinn Fein (with a regrettable degree of cover from the SDLP). Against this, victims and survivors in many cases were increasingly suspicious about the reasons given to justify delays in holding inquests or who question the quality of investigations by the PSNI involving some 'Troubles' type incidents. These concerns were matched by recurring comments from audience members who felt that the pursuit of further investigations and renewed enquiries into past events which were now decades old simply served to poison the political climate so that 'a line should be drawn' and these issues no longer pursued.

In this last context, Anne Graham, sister of Edgar Graham the brilliant young Queen's University law lecturer who was brutally murdered in December 1983 as he went about his university day, made a memorable comment at the Conference when she explained how her family had learned little or nothing from the investigation of the murder and, unhappily, she had reached the conclusion that little point was now being served in continuing the process.

And so to the readers of the papers now published here. While the issues bristle with complication (and not a little risk) there is need to bear in mind the human tragedy which lies behind so much of 'The Past' as well as the baleful influence it can exert. Jeffrey Dudgeon certainly deserves our congratulations for having organised this important Conference.

Brian Garrett

Contents

Introductory Remarks

Councillor Jeffrey Dudgeon MBE

Legacy Legislation Conference

Malone House

3 March 2018

A warm welcome to you all despite the snow. This audience is certainly sturdier than Belfast City Council which cancelled its Thursday meeting despite being due to discuss Brexit, abortion and an Irish Language Act. It will now be on Monday night and livestreamed, if anyone should want to start viewing Belfast's only representative assembly.

I am sorry so many can't be here today, being are out of the country but they have given their support to the event: I name a few: Peter Sheridan, Arthur Aughey, Richard English and David Hoey. Although some of those apologising have been stuck in Belfast and have now managed to make it.

Sadly our first speaker in the afternoon, Austen Morgan, has been stranded in London after his flight was cancelled. His paper is on most seats and his PowerPoint will be presented at speed later.

Doug Beattie is unfortunately ill but we have replaced him as a speaker with Dr William Matchett, the author, who has kindly stepped in at very short notice.

Brian Garrett is here to facilitate when I sit down and I thank him mightily for that. His skills at arbitration are well recognised.

There are many themes for discussion today and I will allude briefly to some.

This event was planned as early as November in anticipation of the London Government releasing its extensive Legacy Bill for enactment by Westminster. I gather it runs to over a hundred pages, with innumerable job opportunities thereafter for staffing the proposed bodies if they emerge. I doubt they or any of it will be time-limited to the notional five years.

The Bill remains unpublished. The consultation has not started but we are advised that the consultation will be about implementation.

As Lord Empey has made clear, there are concerns about Secretary of State, Karen Bradley saying she will be "consulting on how to implement the Stormont House legacy institutions as soon as possible". Not consulting on the content of the Bill, not whether it should be enacted, but only how it should be put into effect.

In January 2014, many of us met here to discuss the recently collapsed Haass talks.

I was somewhat surprised at their disintegration and none were more crestfallen than Richard Haass and Meghan O'Sullivan.

They had come close to a resolution of the Parading issue but not to the other aspects of the Past and Flags.

Within a year, Peter Robinson and Naomi Long who, between them, ensured Haass's efforts appeared to go nowhere had been happy to endorse the Stormont House Agreement with all the worst aspects of the report on the Past included.

Haass had succeeded but it was too late for him to gain any credit.

My party did not agree the Stormont House Agreement. In fact only the DUP and SF did despite the deceptive word 'agreement'. Not unlike that horridly deceptive 'international human rights standards' phrase. But out of it has come the Legacy Bill.

Oddly, the security files, and access to them, were the stumbling blocks previously when Martin McGuinness vetoed progress. And London will hold the line to a large degree over the files but little else, as Haass advised.

That unseen but enormous Legacy Bill must not be implemented without the chance of considerable amendment, or even proposed institutions being scrapped, during a genuine consultation. Without our voices being heard, that is unlikely.

We are not a petty people, this mixture of liberals, civil libertarians unionists and non-unionists who value freedom and human rights – the right to life in particular.

Academic freedom is a key subject, dear to many of our hearts but it takes different forms. There can be little real freedom if one view monopolises our two universities' law schools, under the title transitional justice. What's wrong with justice? The Academy is clearly unbalanced.

Last weekend's *Time for Truth* march and rally in the city centre, attended by the Alliance Party, was an indication of the level of rage out there. The black flags do not augur well for the future.

And it is that rage which concerns me most. The problem with rewriting the history of the past, thus giving moral equivalence to the paramilitaries, concerns the future not the past. Its use is to energise generations to come through myths, emotion, and exaggeration. And that will bring war again.

Victims responded in so many ways: a large number were silent or impressively forgiving, concentrating then and since on facing up to their loss and dealing as best they could with a diminished future.

A smaller number steeled themselves to be public with their concerns, and to campaign for justice, and to assist in creating a stable peace. Some of them are here today.

I think often of the over 700 soldiers who were killed in action (and the amazing figure of 700 from other causes such as accidents and suicides).

For most of their families there was little truth or justice. A 20-minute inquest was then standard, with little evidence beyond the medical. The wives and parents in Britain were baffled and often overwhelmed. Then they were ignored. Even commemoration was limited and strictly regimental.

Our conference is necessary to re-open a debate that was never opened in the first place. The arrangements for the Past are shrouded in mystery and dogma such as the European Convention on Human Rights (ECHR) and Article 2 'compliance'.

Article 2 of the ECHR is about the right to life but should concern more than the state something government does not grasp.

Article 2 needs broken open and debated. However the Foreign Office which seems to hire the most docile of lawyers operates on obfuscation and delay rather than head-on dispute. And the costs mount up and the time.

We aim to change that at Malone House by developing a new consensus on alternative ways to address the past, ones that can bring peace of mind to the victims and justice, so far as that is possible.

There has to be a time limit to re-opening inquests, for example, but there is no chance of one while the current beliefs and arrangements at the NIO, in particular, predominate.

Indeed every inquest on every one of the 3,700 victims can be re-opened given current criteria. And then re-opened again. Article 2, as interpreted, guarantees centuries-long litigation. The only legacy beneficiaries will be lawyers while the chance of real politics reappearing at Stormont are ever more drastically diminished.

About the author

Jeffrey Dudgeon MBE was the plaintiff at the European Court of Human Rights in Strasbourg whose 1981 judgement led to the decriminalisation of male homosexuality in Northern Ireland. He is the author of Roger Casement: *The Black Diaries – With a Study of his Background, Sexuality, and Irish Political Life* (2002). A second, extended edition was published in 2016 alongside *Roger Casement: The German Diary 1914-1916.* He is also the author of *H. Montgomery Hyde - Ulster Unionist MP, Gay Law Reform Campaigner and Prodigious Author* (2018). Jeff was one of the Ulster Unionist Party's two negotiators at the 2013 Haass Talks on the issues of Flags, Parades and the Past. He was elected in 2014 as an Ulster Unionist for the Balmoral DEA on Belfast City Council.

Jeff Dudgeon in front of Belfast City Hall

Legacy needs overhaul that Stormont House bodies will not bring

NL 28|3|18

Recently the Irish deputy prime minister Simon Coveney met victims and survivors, and then called for "urgent progress" on legacy.

Mr Coveney, who is never slow to tell Britain what it must do, then said Ireland would help push along the Stormont House Agreement legacy structures. He seemed to be trying to make clear that Ireland was being constructive, as well as prodding other participants.

The problem is that almost every day there are fresh grounds to believe that the approach to the legacy of the Troubles needs an overhaul the Stormont House bodies will not bring.

Far from funding a raft of legacy inquests, which Mr Coveney again demanded after his meeting and Sinn Fein also demands (no wonder, given that many of the dead are terrorists killed by the state), we need to pause completely on legacy.

It was confirmed yesterday that two elderly soldiers will face trial for shooting an IRA murderer.

Meanwhile, there no outward sign of progress in being made in bringing IRA leaders to trial.

Meanwhile, 'collusion' is still defined in a way that delights republicans, as they continue to spray allegations of it.

Meanwhile, the PSNI legacy branch is swamped with historic investigations, disproportionately into the state (the last figures showed 30% of the probes were into the a state that was behind 10% of Troubles killings, overwhelmingly legitimate).

The recent decision to fund a private civil case against the Hyde Park bombers but the failure of victims of the IRA Birmingham mass murderers to get the same, show that things can be done — and they must be done, given that republicans are so cocky on legacy they have made of Stormont House implementation central to return of devolution.

As for the Irish Republic, given that it took a 'hooded men' case that was rejected at Strasbourg, it is time the UK finally starts referring to Ireland's extradition refusals of IRA murderers that made Margaret Thatcher realise she had made a huge blunder in giving a Dublin a say in Northern Ireland.

Belfast News Letter, Morning View, 28 March 2018

Misconceptions on 'Truth & Justice' – an Overview

Neil Faris, Solicitor, Belfast

Preface

The *Stormont House Agreement* in para 21 proclaims its adherence to various principles, in its approach to dealing with the past. These are stated to include:

- upholding the rule of law;
- facilitating the pursuit of justice and information recovery;
- being 'human rights compliant'; and
- that the approach to the past should be 'balanced, proportionate, transparent, fair and equitable'.

In reality, the proposals now being made flout all these principles to a very worrying extent.

Our leaders have seen fit to sign up to processes which involve or may involve the violation of the rights of those on whom these processes would focus.

The most telling way to approach the many unacceptable proposals is to ask why then these leaders predicate their political claims on, often invalid, assertions that these are 'rights based'?

Starting with the reporting mechanisms, it is unacceptable that those to whom the contents of reports would or may be highly prejudicial may not have enjoyed the right to legal representation and cross examination and to see all relevant documents before any adjudication could fairly be made.

At the same time, there must be an independent adjudicating tribunal which must be both patently impartial and also experienced in making adjudications of such importance.

The demand for procedural fairness involving observing the rules of natural justice could not be rejected by anyone whose purpose is other than stigmatising for political ends.

It follows inexorably from the above that the tribunal making any kind of 'assessment' on the conduct of any individual must be susceptible to judicial review in the High Court, otherwise there can be no certainty that the requirements of procedural fairness set out in this Paper will be met.

Furthermore, human right protection for a person's reputation must not be over-ridden. The European Court of Human Right has protected reputation under Article 8 of the European Convention on Human Rights: imparting information that a person has committed a criminal offence interferes with the right to private life if the person in question has not been convicted. Thus the proposals for the legacy bodies to issue reports implicating any individual in circumstances where there has been no conviction will be in breach of Article 8 of the Convention.

It is true that a by-product of insistence on the insertion into the legacy legislation of proper human rights provisions would be that those who have perpetuated violence would benefit as well as the innocent. But that is the nature of justice.

So this Paper proceeds on the basis that the protection and burden of the law must apply to all: whatever their 'role' may have been during the Troubles.

But there is a further disturbing element in the proposed legacy legislation. The police will be singled out for investigation in cases of alleged 'misconduct' where there is no question of a breach of the criminal law having occurred. This 'misconduct' investigatory process will be imposed on retired police officers, now 'civilians' like the rest of us. This is clearly a retrospective change in their terms of service and is discriminatory, as such retired police officers will be the only category of those involved in the Troubles against whom any finding of 'misconduct' will be made, in circumstances where they are not guilty of any criminal offence. It is simply contrary to the 'rule of law'[1] for such penalty provisions to be applied retrospectively to the terms of service of police officers who have retired.

The only reasonable conclusion is that the Talks Participants in these proposals are seeking to warp justice for their various political ends. This Paper challenges that.

Without the acceptance of the principles set out in this Paper it is highly likely that it is the innocent who will suffer most.

Finally, it has to be clearly understood that, despite the complexity of what is proposed and the very substantial public funding that will have to be committed for the entire duration of the process, there will be only a partial investigation: the focus is on 'Troubles-related deaths'. All other aspects of the Troubles will receive either no, or only passing, mention.

This can only lead to an enduring sense of injustice on the part of those who have suffered in all other aspects of the Troubles but who will feel ignored in the entire legacy process.

---

[1] See further below, section 7.

Executive Summary

I apologise that this paper is dense and detailed. But on the one hand there is simply no other way to give any proper scrutiny of the elaborate proposals, as sketched out in the various documents which I have examined. On the other hand, one must then apply the various principles of justice to what is proposed. When such scrutiny is carried out, the defects of the proposals come to light.

I acknowledge, with thanks, the considerable help of Peter Smith CBE, QC in the preparation of this paper, but any responsibility rests with me.

- *Part One – Introduction*

    1. Section 1 'The Basic Structure' lists the various bodies that the Talks Parties propose to establish.

    2. Section 2 'Overview': this contains two sub-sections:

        o *The Reporting Mechanisms* identifies the central importance that the issue of Reports will have in the process;

        o *The Human Rights protection of reputation* sets out the essential human rights protection, which appears to have been ignored by the Talks Participants.

- *Part Two – the New Institutions*

    3. Section 3 The Historical Investigations Unit ('HIU');

4. Section 4 The Independent Commission on Information Retrieval ('ICIR');

5. Section 5 The Oral History Archive ('OHA'); and

6. Section 6 The Implementation and Reconciliation Group ('IRG').

- *Part Three – the Underlying Principles*

7. Section 7 'The Rule of Law';

8. Section 8 'Natural Justice'; and

9. Section 9 'Examples from the Courts': this contains two sub-sections:

   o *The Loughinisland judicial review* refers to the recent judicial review judgment of Mr Justice McCloskey; and

   o *Robbery and Death at Ashford, County Wicklow* is a pertinent example of how an independent investigation into a death with 'state actor' involvement can be thoroughly and fairly carried out.

- *Part Four – Police 'Misconduct'*

10. Section 10 is justified as a separate section as what is planned for retired police officers seems to me to reek of injustice.

- *Part Five – Conclusions*

Part One – Introduction

1. The Basic Structure

1.1 Four new institutions are proposed to investigate and report on the past, albeit that only Troubles-related deaths will be given any detailed consideration.

1.2 The actual proposals (contained apparently in a draft Bill) are still under concealment by the two main Northern Ireland parties and the two Governments (collectively the 'Talks Participants'[2], notwithstanding that 'talks' have been proceeding since 2014.

1.3 Nevertheless, it is possible to glean a degree of detail from documents such as the *Stormont House Agreement* of 23 December 2014, a Department of Justice *Position Paper and Stakeholder Engagement Workshop* of 6 August 2015 and certain other paperwork to which I shall refer as we go along. (The *Fresh Start Agreement* of 17 November 2015 is altogether too coy to give any further information at all!)

1.4 The institutions are to be: The *Historical Investigations Unit* – this will re-consider a selected list of Troubles-related deaths;

- The *Independent Commission on Information Retrieval* – this has already been established by treaty between the

---

[2] I recognise that, technically at least, the other parties who have participated in the Executive are also talks participants, but it is apparent from media reports and their own statements that they have not been in any real sense in the negotiations for many months – so for the purposes of this paper 'Talks Participants' means the two main parties and their advisors and the two governments and their civil servants/diplomats.

United Kingdom and Irish governments. Its function will be to enable victims and survivors privately to receive information about the Troubles-related deaths of their next of kin;

- The *Oral History Archive* – this will be an oral history archive which will receive and store accounts of personal experiences during the course of the Troubles;

- The *Implementation and Reconciliation Group* – this will be established 'to oversee themes, archives and information recovery'[3]. It will commission a report on 'themes' from independent academic experts.

1.5 In following sections I shall set out a brief resume of the available evidence on the intentions of the Talks Participants for each of these new institutions.

1.6 As we go along, it will become apparent that the whole investigatory scheme is based on a hierarchy of reporting mechanisms. In brief:

- The HIU will issue Reports upwards to the IRG;

- The ICIR will produce Reports to victims' families and will also submit to the IRG a report on 'patterns and themes';

- The OHA must also produce to the IRG a Report on 'patterns and themes' in all the oral history it collects;

- Armed with all these Reports the IRG then appoints an Academic Panel to prepare a report on 'patterns and themes'.

1.7 If Reports are to be produced, implicating individuals in criminal activity or imputing misconduct, then specific

---

[3] *Stormont House Agreement,* para 51.

and essential principles of justice must be observed. It is very worrying that, in the available documentation, there does not appear to be any definite acknowledgement of these principles nor any specific confirmation of how the principles are to be observed in the reporting activities of each of the new bodies.

1.8 So in section 2 of this part of the Paper I give a brief resume of what seem to me to be the bare minimum of the relevant principles. Then Part Two gives a resume of the available detail of the new bodies and that is followed in Part Three with further treatment of the essential justice principles so that the reader may measure how, if at all, any of the new bodies will adequately observe the principles and protect individual rights.

2. Overview

- *The Reporting Mechanisms*

2.1 I set out some overview points:

- While all such investigation and reporting can, in theory at least, apply to the actions of those who have perpetuated violence (both republican and loyalist), the actuality is that the focus will be on the actions of the police and security forces, if only because of the bulk of archive material that will be available to the investigators from public sources, compared with the minimal amount of archive material of any usable quality that will be available from other 'private' sources.

- Reports can be very damaging to the reputations of individuals. (I deal with the specific human rights protection of reputation in the next subsection). It will be retired police officers and other retired members of the armed forces who will bear the brunt of the investigations.

- One would only hope that the Talks Participants have fully recognised this important principle of natural justice and that the draft Bill will contain full safeguards for the rights and reputations of <u>all</u> those who are investigated and whose actions are commented on in the raft of reports. If the draft Bill contains no such specific protective measures then it will be the vehicle for great injustice – the peace process will be contaminated for another generation.

- *The Human Rights protection of reputation*

2.2 Article 8 of the European Convention on Human Rights provides for a right to 'respect for private and family life ...' This has been interpreted by the European Court of Human Rights in Strasbourg to include protection of reputation: in particular, imparting information that a person has committed a criminal offence interferes with the right to private life if the person in question has not been convicted.

2.3 It appears that this applies even where the allegation has not been made publicly available[4]. Thus it must follow that the proposed disclosure to victims of findings of fact amounting to determinations of guilt other than by a court of competent jurisdiction (i.e. a criminal court) would constitute breach of Article 8.

2.4 Thus, unless the draft Bill fully and properly protects 'rep-

---

[4] *Mikolajova v. Slovakia* Application no. 4479/03, judgment dated 18 January 2011.

utation' in accordance with Article 8 of the European Convention on Human Rights, it will fall to be struck down in the Courts for 'incompatibility' under the *Human Rights Act 1998*.

2.5   This must preclude the provision of reports to victims identifying alleged perpetrators (of any category). But assuming that the Talks Participants are determined to proceed in defiance of the Article 8 provisions to protect reputation, then the real risk arises of victims disclosing their identities by way of 'leak'. For this, the only remedy would be via the courts. Effective provision would have to be made in the legislation. Generally, the only way that the rights of putative perpetrators could be protected would be by way of judicial review so the suggestion that judicial review might be prohibited in certain circumstances in the draft Bill must be resisted at all costs.

2.6   But even here there is a problem. Just as reporting restrictions on trials in Northern Ireland are not enforceable in our neighbouring jurisdiction, how could alleged perpetrators be protected against press reports in that jurisdiction based on 'leaks'?

2.7   I now set out some available detail on the proposed new institutions.

Part Two - The New Institutions

3. The Historical Investigations Unit

3.1   Some preliminary detail is contained in paras 30 to 40 of the Stormont House Agreement. The HIU is to take forward outstanding cases from the HET process[5] and the

---

[5]   The *Historic Enquiries Team* of the Police Service of Northern Ireland

legacy work of the Police Ombudsman for Northern Ireland ('the Police Ombudsman').

3.2   A Report will be produced on each case and the process is to be 'victim centred' including provision of a dedicated family support staff who will provide the next of kin with 'expert advice and other necessary support throughout the process'[6]: no equivalent provision mentioned for any of those under investigation.

3.3   It appears, though not clearly set out in the Stormont House Agreement, that the first function of HIU in any case will to be to carry out a criminal investigation and 'as with existing criminal investigations', the decision to prosecute is for the DPP and the HIU may consult the DPP's office on evidentiary issues in advance of submitting a file.

3.4   In the case of such criminal investigations the HIU will have full policing powers: presumably also the concomitant policing duties and safeguards such as PACE, though the Stormont House Agreement does not deem such as worthy of mention[7].

3.5   There is to be provision for co-operation with the Republic of Ireland, including disclosure of information and documentation and arrangements for obtaining evidence for use in court proceedings. (The Irish Government is to bring forward additional legislation where such is required.) It is not clear if this 'co-operation' is to extend to

---

was instituted to carry out a review of all the unsolved Troubles-related deaths. But it was subject to attack for alleged non-compliance with Article 2 of the *European Convention on Human Rights* and consequently abandoned.

[6]   *Stormont House Agreement*, para 33.

[7]   But see further para 3.8 5th bullet, below.

cases where, when prosecution is not possible, HIU issues Reports to the families. How will such information from the Republic be handled for proper protection of those to whom the Reports relate?

3.6   It is not clearly stated in the *Stormont House Agreement* what happens in circumstances where there is insufficient evidence to mount a prosecution: very surprising as it is generally accepted that very few prosecutions may result. However, the Department of Justice Position Paper and Stakeholder Engagement Workshop of 6 August 2015 ('the DoJ Paper') states that a Report will be produced in each case: it is not clear to whom the Report is to be issued.

3.7   Para 32 of the *Stormont House Agreement* states that there will be appropriate governance arrangements to ensure the operational independence of the two different elements of the work.

3.8   The DoJ Paper also refers to the following elements which apparently are included in the draft Bill[8]:

- Families may apply to have other cases considered for criminal investigation 'if there is new evidence that was not previously before the HET, and is relevant to the identification and eventual prosecution of the perpetrator'.

- HIU will also have power to conduct investigations regarding 'misconduct' by police where a complaint has been previously made to the Police Ombudsman 'or where evidence of misconduct is uncovered during the course of an investigation or brought to the HIU, and

---

[8]   *DoJ Paper*, para 9.

the case falls within the remit of the HIU"[9]. It appears, as already indicated, and subject to the actual provisions of the draft Bill, that such powers of investigation of 'misconduct' can be wielded against retired police officers. Serious questions arise as to the legitimacy of any such proposal:

- o Why should such retired police officers be subject to such retrospective penal provisions?

- o This must, under the accepted principle of the 'rule of law'[10], be an illegitimate exercise of a retrospective provision against police officers who did not have any such requirement in the their terms of service when they joined either the Royal Ulster Constabulary or the Police Service of Northern Ireland.

- o Furthermore, why are such retired officers, out of all the actors in the Troubles, singled out for such treatment and what protection of their rights will there be?

(Further consideration of this troubling aspect of the legacy proposals in section 10 below)

- In respect of the conduct of <u>criminal investigations</u> into a death within in the remit of the HIU the HIU officers will have the full powers and privileges of police constables.

- In exercising its powers relating to <u>police misconduct investigations</u>, the HIU, will have the equivalent powers to the Police Ombudsman.

---

[9] *DoJ Paper*, para 10.

[10] See section 7 below.

- It is not clear if suspects under HIU <u>criminal investigation</u> will have the full protection of the Police and Criminal Evidence Act ('PACE') as applies to and controls the PSNI in 'ordinary' investigations. There is an opaque reference in the DoJ Paper that 'HIU's detailed powers around the application of ... PACE will be set out in subordinate legislation'[11].

- Furthermore, it is not clear what protection there may be for retired police officers in HIU <u>police misconduct investigations?</u>

- Turning than to the Reports to be produced by HIU, the DoJ Paper states that it is expected that Reports will be provided 'prior to publication':

  o To the family once the investigation is concluded;

  o To the DPP in order to consider the prospects for prosecution;

  o To PSNI/NIPB if there is evidence of misconduct of a serving officer, so that appropriate action can be taken.[12]

So the prospects of 'leaking', perhaps selectively, are legion and when this happens those on whom adverse comment is made in the Report will have no remedy to protect their reputations nor even knowledge of the entire contents of the Report.

The role of the DPP in taking independent decision, as he or she should, in regard to the institution of criminal pro-

---

11 *DoJ Paper*, para 11.
12 *DoJ Paper*, para 19.

ceedings is seriously compromised by this 'pre-publication' process.

- Then 'a version of the Report will be published where appropriate': are there to be any provisions to protect reputations in cases where there is no prosecution followed by conviction in the Courts? This is likely to be a contravention of the protection of reputation under Article 8 of the European Convention on Human Rights[13].

- The HIU will as a public authority act in accordance with legislation such as the Human Rights Act, the Data Protection Act and the Freedom of Information Act[14].

- There is extensive provision for 'Family Support and Engagement' on the part of HIU but no provision for any such support and engagement to be offered to others involved in any HIU investigation.

- The HIU will be a body corporate, established as a Non-Departmental Public Body of the DoJ. It will be overseen by the NIPB in similar fashion as NIPB oversees the PSNI - including operational independence for the HIU in the conduct of investigations.

- The DoJ Paper sketches out some staffing details – space constraints do not allow me to cover these here.

- The DoJ Paper provides that HIU will publish procedures similar to those of the Police Ombudsman in respect of complaints of maladministration on the part of HIU or any of its officers. It notes that any challenge to the outcome of an investigation will be made within

---

[13] See paras 2.2 to 2.4 above.

[14] *DoJ Paper*, para 21.

HIU in the first instance and ultimately through the Courts as currently is the case with the Police Ombudsman.

- But it must have 'a committee to deal with complaints and disciplinary matters with the power to bring in outside persons to participate in order to ensure independent and impartial procedures'[15]. Of course, this all falls far short of transparency and true independence.

- Inspection of HIU will be carried out by the Criminal Justice Inspection Northern Ireland and DoJ or NIPB may also request Her Majesty's Inspectorate of Constabulary to inspect and report on the efficiency and effectiveness of HIU.

3.9   It is also stipulated that 'in order to ensure expeditious investigations the HIU should aim to complete its work within five years of its establishment'[16]. The DoJ Paper clarifies that they do not intend to provide a specific closing date in legislation but there will be a power 'to close the HIU at a later date, once it has completed the work it has been tasked with'[17]. So five years may be optimistic!

4. The Independent Commission on Information Retrieval ('ICIR')

4.1   The Secretary of State (Mrs Theresa Villiers MP, at the time) made a statement in the House of Commons on 21 January 2016. She acknowledged that the two governments 'have signed an agreement to enable the establish-

---

[15] *DoJ Paper*, para 35.

[16] *Stormont House Agreement* para 40.

[17] *DoJ Paper*, para 39.

ment of the ICIR and to set out its functions'. She did not 'lay' the agreement before the House for ratification, on the basis that the debate on it should take place along with consideration of the legislation 'which will contain more detail about how the ICIR will function' (presumably in the draft Bill). However, she stated that the agreement is available in the Parliamentary libraries: but to members of parliament only – not available in web search of the library's website.

4.2 However, her statement does contain the following bare details:

- The ICIR will enable victims and survivors privately to receive information about the Troubles-related deaths of their next of kin. All the reporting problems arise here also: the natural justice requirements giving full challenge rights to those implicated (whether fairly or no) and the protection of reputation rights in all cases where there is no prosecution followed by conviction in the Courts.

- It will be an international body (following the precedent of the Independent Commission on the Location of Victims' Remains);

- Engagement by families with ICIR will be entirely voluntary;

- Information provided to ICIR 'about deaths within its remit' will not be admissible in court – and families will always be told this in advance;

- There will be no amnesty or immunity from prosecution: 'This Government believes in the rule of law and would not countenance such a step.'

4.3   And some more detail is available in paras 41 to 50 of the *Stormont House Agreement*:

- Once established the body will run for no more than five years;

- There will be a chairperson 'who may be of international standing', appointed by the two governments, in consultation with OFMDFM and four other members: two appointed by OFMDFM and one appointed by each government;

- Its remit will cover both jurisdictions and have the same functions in each;

- It will be entirely separate from the justice system. Surely this must not be taken to mean that the natural justice and reputational rights of individuals are to be over-ridden by this 'international' body?

- It will be free to seek information from other jurisdictions and both governments undertake to support such requests;

- It will not disclose information provided to it to law enforcement or intelligence agencies and its information will be inadmissible in criminal and civil proceedings;

- It will be given the immunities and privileges of an international body;

- It will not be subject to judicial review, Freedom of Information, Data Protection and National Archives legislation in either jurisdiction. This seems to answer the above question: the natural justice and reputational rights of individuals are to be over-ridden by this 'international' body!

- However, the problem – which the Talks Participants

do not appear to have identified – is that the protection of reputation of individuals under Article 8 of the European Convention on Human Rights cannot be 'overridden' by the Governments of the United Kingdom and Ireland, acting singly or in collusion.

- It will not disclose the identities of people who provide information but no individual who provides information will be immune from prosecution for any crime committed should the evidential requirements be satisfied by other means;

- It 'will be held accountable to the principles of independence, rigour, fairness and balance, transparency and proportionality'. If the courts are to be excluded to what independent authority will ICIR by 'accountable'? What does accountability entail in these circumstances?

4.4   It is really astonishing that the Talks Participants and those advising them contemplate the immunity of ICIR from accountability to any individual in court by way of judicial review and the over-riding of essential legislative protection, such as Data Protection rights.

4.5   There is no space here to list all the manifest abuse of individual rights that this presents but just to take one example:

If family members request information about the Troubles-related death of their next of kin, an individual may 'confess' to ICIR his or her involvement in such death, and such information may be passed on to the family members.

But if the confession implicates or alleges involvement of others in the death, to what extent can ICIR release such information to the family, other than the bare confession of the confessor – relating to his or her actions only?

ICIR should not under principles of natural justice and protection of reputation (already discussed elsewhere in this paper) release information implicating other individuals without such individuals having right of challenge. I cannot see how this would be feasible without breach of the confidentiality of the confessor?

So in such case the information released by ICIR to the family could be only the bare confession, without implicating others. Quite understandably, family members would then feel there had been 'cover up' by ICIR as it would be in possession of further information from the confessor which was directly relevant to the circumstances of the death of their loved one but which could not properly be released to the family because it implicated others who were not party to the confession?

4.6   I return to the question as to whether the information given to 'victims and survivors' would include allegations against individuals which are unproven in any court?

4.7   As already explained, Article 8 of the *European Convention on Human Rights* would seem to preclude this. But assuming, as appears to be the case, that the Talks Participants are intent on ignoring or overriding the human rights protections which I have mentioned, what alternative mechanisms would be in place to protect the interests of such individuals? By what means would the 'privacy' of information disclosed 'privately' be protected?

4.8   I have already commented above at para 2.6 that Court non-disclosure orders made in Northern Ireland are ineffective outside our jurisdiction.

4.9   Furthermore, it would be impossible, in face of the press tradition of non-disclosure, to trace the family member who 'leaked'. So effective protection would be impossible and the 'leak' would inevitably go viral on social media.

4.10 The individual fingered and targeted in such 'leak' would apparently be deprived of the remedy of suit for defamation against ICIR in respect of its report, because ICIR is to have the immunities and privileges of an international body.

4.11 Certainly, I have already remarked on the grand declaration of the 'accountability' of ICIR to 'the principles of independence, rigour, fairness and balance, transparency and proportionality'. But absent the scrutiny of the judiciary in Belfast and Dublin by way of judicial review, how is ICIR, as an international institution, actually to be held to account?

4.12 Perhaps, the draft Bill will resolve all?

Marino Branch
Brainse Marino
Tel: 8336297

5. The Oral History Archive

5.1 The *Stormont House Agreement* gives some detail in paras 22 to 25:

- The Archive is to be established by the Executive 'by 2016'.

- It is 'to provide a central place for people from all backgrounds (and throughout the UK and Ireland) to share experiences and narratives related to the Troubles'.

- It is to be run on an entirely voluntary basis.

- Consideration to be given to protecting the participants and the body itself from defamation claims.

- The Archive will bring forward proposals on the circumstances and timing of contributions being made public.

- It will be independent and free from political interference.

- A research project will be established as part of the Archive 'led by academics to produce a factual historical timeline and statistical analysis of the Troubles to report within 12 months'.

5.2   All seems to me to be self-evidently so inherently absurd, so ludicrously naÃ¯ve and so lacking in analytical thought, as not really to require further comment.

5.3   But just to raise two simple questions:

- How are those against whom allegations are made in such oral history 'narratives', expressly or by implication, to protect themselves?

- Why should those making malicious allegations in such 'narratives' be protected against defamation claims?

5.4   I merely observe the poignancy of the express proclamations of the *Stormont House Agreement* to upholding the rule of law, being human rights compliant' and that the approach to the past should be 'balanced, proportionate, transparent, fair and equitable'.

6. The Implementation and Reconciliation Group

6.1   The *Stormont House Agreement* gives some detail in paras 51 to 55 (I have set this out in more logical sequence):

- The chair shall be a person of independent and international standing nominated by the OFMDFM.

- There will be eight nominations from Northern Ireland political parties as follows: DUP three nominees; Sinn Fein two nominees; SDLP one nominee; UUP one nominee; Alliance Party one nominee[18].

---

18   This dates back to December 2014 and perhaps the electoral arith-

- The United Kingdom government will have one nominee and the Government of Ireland will have one nominee.

- Publicly elected representatives will not be eligible for appointment. (Note that this does not preclude nominations of party members or supporters.)

- The IRG will be established 'to oversee themes, archives and information recovery'.

- Any potential evidence base for patterns and themes should be referred to the IRG from any of the legacy mechanisms.

- They may 'comment on the level of co-operation received'.

- The IRG is to carry out 'analysis and assessment'.

- 'The process should be conducted with sensitivity and rigorous intellectual integrity, devoid of any political interference'.

- After five years it will commission a Report from independent academic experts.

- Promoting reconciliation will underlie all of the work of the IRG. It will encourage and support other initiatives that contribute to reconciliation, better understanding of the past and reducing sectarianism.

- 'In the context of the work of the IRG the UK and Irish Governments will consider statements of acknowledgment and would expect others to do the same.'

6.2   The UK and Irish Governments also acknowledge that there are outstanding investigations and allegations

metic has changed since then?

into Troubles-related incidents, including a number of cross-border incidents. They commit to co-operation with all bodies involved to enable their effective operation, recognising their distinctive functions and to bring forward legislation where necessary.

6.3   Again, I raise some simple questions:

- What analysis of any value could a body so chosen by the conflicting parties ever perform?

- 'Patterns and themes' inevitably involve the conduct of people.

- How could evidence of the same be processed in a manner that would protect individuals? and

- What would be the value of a Report from academic experts chosen in this political fashion and working within the political constraints of the *Stormont House Agreement*?

6.4   It is really a matter well beyond legal analysis as to whether all this will operate as a 'truth recovery process' and as to whether any 'truth recovery' it produces will aid or set back 'reconciliation, better understanding of the past and reducing sectarianism'. So I am happy to leave all that for debate by others.

6.5   I now move to what seem to me to be underlying principles of the importance of the rule of law, natural justice and the promotion of reconciliation that should have motivated and guided the Talks Participants: to anticipate what I go on to set out it seems to me either that they fail to appreciate such principles or are willing to give them lip service only.

Part Three – the Underlying Principles

7. The Rule of Law

7.1   In all the documentation from the Talks Participants referred to in this Paper sadly there is no highlighting of the importance of the observance of the rule of law as an underlying principle to govern the actions of all the legacy institutions. We shall have to await the publication of the draft Bill to see if there has been any progress on this.

7.2   It seems to me that the best definition of the rule of law, at least for practical purposes is that given by the late Tom Bingham[19] in his book *The Rule of Law*[20]

"The core of the existing principle is, I suggest, that all persons and authorities within the state, whether public or private, should be bound by and entitled to the benefit of laws publicly made, taking effect (generally) in the future and publicly administered in the courts."[21]

7.3   Here are two examples from the above narrative of how the Talks Participants appear willing to flout the principles of the rule of law, so defined:

- At para 3.8 above I pointed to the intention to confer

---

[19]   Although he held, successively, the high judicial offices of Master of the Rolls, Lord Chief Justice of England and Wales and Senior Law Lord of the United Kingdom (the only person to hold all three offices) he published as plain 'Tom Bingham'. And his book is in clear English: everyone should read it.

[20]   Penguin Books, London, 2011.

[21]   *Ibid* p. 8

power on the HIU to investigate retired police officers for 'misconduct' uncovered in the course of an HIU investigation of a Troubles-related death. Now, when an officer entered service it was on the basis that he or she was subject to police discipline during service but that on retirement the officer was no longer subject to disciplinary processes, though of course, like every citizen, amenable to the criminal law. It seems to me to run contrary to the rule of law for legislation to be enacted to subject retired officers to this HIU regime when this did not apply in their years of service.

- Secondly, as pointed out in para 4.3 (8th bullet), the ICIR will not be subject to judicial review, Freedom of Information, Data Protection and National Archives legislation in either jurisdiction. So to oust the jurisdiction of our courts runs defiantly counter to the principle of the rule of law that everyone should be:

> ... *entitled to the benefit of laws publicly made ... and publicly administered in the courts*

8. Natural Justice

8.1   As already identified[22], the Talks Participants propose a hierarchy of Reports:

- The HIU will issue Reports upwards to the IRG;

- The HIU will produce Reports to victims' families and will also submit to the IRG a Report on 'patterns and themes';

- The OHA must also produce to the IRG a Report on 'patterns and themes' in all the oral history it collects;

---

[22] Para 1.6 above.

- Armed with all these Reports the IRG then appoints an Academic Panel to prepare a report on 'patterns and themes'

- And as just mentioned in para 7.3 above, while the focus is purportedly on investigation of and reporting on criminal activity concerning any death, the police will face further investigation in respect of 'misconduct'.

8.2   All of this replete with the danger of bias and injustice to individuals unless they have rights of full participation in the adjudicatory process.

8.3   Fortunately, we can draw examples of how this is to be properly, fairly, tackled both from our High Court in Belfast and from the High Court in Dublin.

9. Examples from the Courts

- *The Loughinisland judicial review*

9.1   The recent Loughinisland judicial review[23] was a challenge by retired police officers to adverse comments made by the Police Ombudsman in his Report (otherwise called his 'Public Statement') in regard to the police investigation of the notorious sectarian murders perpetuated at the Heights Bar, Loughinisland, County Down on Saturday evening,18 June 1994.

9.2   Mr Justice McCloskey clearly set out how this should be fairly done:

"... Where the Police Ombudsman, acting within the confines of his statutory powers, proposes to promulgate a 'public statement' which is critical of or otherwise adverse to certain persons four fundamental requirements, rooted

---

[23] *In the matter of an Application by Thomas Ronald Hawthorne and Raymond White for Judicial Review* [2018] NIQB 5.

in common law fairness, must be observed. First, all passages of the draft report impinging directly or indirectly on the affected individuals must be disclosed to them, accompanied by an invitation to make representations. Second, a reasonable period for making such representations must be permitted. Third, any representations received must be the product of conscientious consideration on the part of the Police Ombudsman, entailing an open mind and a genuine willingness to alter and/or augment the draft report. Finally, the response of the individual concerned must be fairly and accurately portrayed in the report which enters the public domain."[24]

9.3   Just to summarise the fundamental requirements which <u>as a minimum</u> must be observed in any investigatory and reporting process:

- Where a report is to be made which is critical of or otherwise adverse to certain persons *four fundamental requirements*, rooted in common law fairness, must be observed.

- *First*, all passages of the draft report impinging directly or indirectly on the affected individuals must be disclosed to them, accompanied by an invitation to make representations.

---

[24] Para 114. Note that by reason of a 'recusal' challenge McCloskey J determined that the matter should be reheard before another judge and because of this he held [para 188 (iii)]:
   "The judgment of this court will be neither binding on any party nor executory in nature. It will not bind a future court. It will, rather, assume a hybrid status, somewhat akin to an advisory opinion, which features in legal systems other than ours"
In any event, it seems to me that para 114 is a statement of 'good law'.

- *Second*, a reasonable period for making such representations must be permitted.

- *Third*, any representations received must be the product of conscientious consideration on the part of the person preparing the report, entailing an open mind and a genuine willingness to alter and/or augment the draft report.

- *Finally*, the response of the individual concerned must be fairly and accurately portrayed in the report which enters the public domain."

9.4   It remains to be seen how these four fundamental principles are to be properly and fairly observed and implemented in all the reporting hierarchy of the proposed legacy legislation.

9.5   One recent example of how this can be properly and fairly done is available from a recent judgment of the Dublin High Court.

- *Robbery & death at Ashford, County Wicklow*

9.6   On 1st May 1998 a gang (apparently Real IRA members) were planning to carry out an armed robbery on a cash-in-transit van in Ashford. But the robbers' two vans had themselves been under gardai surveillance. Thirty members of the Garda National Surveillance Unit were on the scene, and the raid was thwarted. One of the gang members, Ronan MacLochlainn (28 years of age), attempted to escape in a hi-jacked car but three Garda NSU officers shot at MacLochlainn and he was fatally wounded.[25]

---

[25] The officer who fired the fatal shot made a statement at the time but subsequently died.

9.7   Mr MacLochlainn's partner, Grainne Nic Gibb, through her solicitor, claimed that "gardai could have stopped the attempted robbery beforehand and arrested MacLochlainn but instead 'went for the spectacular'."[26]

9.8   This is of course redolent of allegations of 'shoot to kill', so I suggest it is relevant to show what were the follow up investigatory processes in our neighbouring jurisdiction in respect of this incident.

9.9   The initial investigation was carried out by a Detective Chief Inspector and Chief Superintendent and an inquest was held in 2010. Of course, the Garda investigation did not meet the requirements of Article 2 of the European Convention on Human Rights for independent investigation when a death occurs as a result of action of the state (in this case that of the Garda officer who shot Mr MacLochlainn and the surrounding circumstances of the Garda action at the scene).

9.10 Accordingly, Ms Nic Gibb subsequently made application to the European Court of Human Rights under Article 2. However, the Irish Government gave an undertaking to the Court that a fully independent investigation would be carried out and the Court accordingly struck out the application.

9.11 Consequently, the Government appointed an independent Commission of enquiry carried out by Mary Rose Gearty SC who heard 60 days of evidence and then issued a draft report. Submissions were made to the Commission on the draft report on behalf of Ms Nic Gibb. Ms Gearty then issued her amended Report on 13 May 2016. In the Report

---

[26] *Irish Times* 17 February 2018 'Judge refuses to overturn verdict of lawful killing'.

it was accepted that there was a conflict of evidence (on the position of the green Mazda vehicle hi-jacked by Ronan MacLochlainn at the time a garda vehicle overtook it) and that it was not possible to resolve this conflict of evidence.

9.12 The legislation under which the enquiry was held entitled Ms Nic Gibb to make application to the High Court in Dublin in respect of the findings in Ms Gearty's Report. Ms Nic Gibb duly made such application. She asked the Court 'to delete the Commission's finding of lawful killing from its May 2016 final Report on the basis that it was unsafe because of the Commission's alleged failure to address a range of issues and unexplained gaps in the evidence'[27].

9.13 The matter was heard before Ms Justice Mary Flaherty who considered the Report and the submissions of Ms Nic Gibb[28] and reserved judgment. She handed down her judgment (98 pages) on 16 February last. She held 'she was not persuaded, in finding that the killing was lawful, that the Commission failed to have regard to expert evidence concerning the conduct of the Garda operation and that the assessment of such evidence was for the Commission and not for the Court'[29]. She also concluded that there was no procedural frailty to require the Court to direct the Commission to amend its final Report or to take further evidence.

9.14 These examples demonstrate how it is possible to institute fair procedures to protect the reputations of individuals.

---

[27] *Ibid.*

[28] Neither the Garda Commissioner nor Ms Gearty, a notice party, were represented.

[29] *Irish Times* 17 February 2018 'Judge refuses to overturn verdict of lawful killing' – the full judgment is not yet available.

Part Four

10. Police 'Misconduct'

10.1 Before my Conclusions, I revert to how the police are apparently to be singled out in the proposals by the Talks Participants.

10.2 As I have already indicated if we really strive for justice the only way to proceed is by strict adherence to the principle that the benefit and protection of the law must apply to all, regardless to any perceived rank, occupation or status in society. So all must be subject to the criminal law.

10.3 These principles apply of course to retired police officers as they apply to any section of society.

10.4 But why then are retired police offices to be singled out for investigation for 'misconduct' in cases where no criminal charges are to be brought against them? Apparently, no other section of society is to be subject to 'misconduct' investigations, when no criminal charges are to be brought against them.

10.5 It is difficult to conceive how proposals so redolent with unfairness can possible be perceived as being 'balanced, proportionate, transparent, fair and equitable' (in the final words of para 21 of the *Stormont House Agreement*).

10.6 The proposals will work with particular unfairness against retired police officers (as compared with serving police officers) for the following reasons:

- If an investigation is criminal in nature then the retired officer will have the full protection of all the provisions (such as PACE) which apply for everyone;

- But what protections are there to be when HIU is carrying out a 'misconduct' investigation against a retired police officer?

- What is to be the definition of 'misconduct'?

- In the case where a prosecution is initiated then the accused has the vital protection that the charge or charges must be proved beyond reasonable doubt before an independent court.

- The accused has full rights of challenge to all evidence being presented to the Court with concomitant duties on the prosecutor to act with full fairness and propriety in presenting the evidence and conducting the prosecution in every aspect.

- The accused, if convicted, has right of appeal to a higher, also independent, court.

- If a 'misconduct' allegation is made against a serving police officer then it must be shown that he or she is in breach of specific disciplinary regulations/code of conduct.

- Such serving officer has the right to a hearing before an independent disciplinary tribunal which must observe the rules of evidence.

- The officer has full rights of challenge to all evidence being presented to the Tribunal which must be satisfied beyond all reasonable doubt.

- The officer may also avail of appeal rights if the charge is proven.

- But a retired officer is a mere civilian so is not entitled to the process and protections in respect of the disciplinary investigations of serving officers.

- It appears that under the current procedure of the Police Ombudsman such <u>retired</u> officers are interviewed as 'witnesses' but as such are not entitled to the full protective measures which are available to anyone who faces a criminal charge or to the protective measures which are available to <u>serving</u> officers who face a disciplinary investigation.

10.7 How is all this patent unfairness to be addressed?

Part Five

11. Conclusion

11.1 It seems to me that it is essential for a detailed, rigorous investigatory and reporting process to be put in place before any investigation of Troubles-related deaths proceeds.

11.2 Everyone implicated, or likely to be implicated, in such investigatory and reporting processes (officers of the police, the family of the deceased person and all others however involved or implicated) is entitled to the benefit and protection of such detailed process.

11.3 Will all this be duly and transparently set out in the Consultation Document on the draft Bill to be issued sometime soon?

11.4 Or are the Talks Participants content with 'justice on the cheap' as their proposals to date seem to suggest?

11.5 Are they oblivious to, or unappreciative of, the harm they may cause to innocent individuals if they fail to adopt such thorough but fair investigatory and reporting processes as were clearly demonstrated in the sad case of the death of Ronan MacLochlainn?

11.6 For the various reasons set out in this Paper, it does seem to me that the Talks Participants' proposals are simply not fit for purpose and should be abandoned.

About the author

Neil Faris is currently a solicitor in independent practice specialising in public and commercial law, expert conveyancing reports, advisory and research work.

'"The Possibilities are Endless": Republican Strategy to Deal with the Past and Transitional Justice in Northern Ireland'

Dr Cillian McGrattan

Ulster University

This paper explores some of the political dynamics surrounding the legacy legislation debate in Northern Ireland. It suggests that the Provisional republican narrative about the past will remain self-serving, self-exculpatory; it will continue to focus on structural assertions to deflect from individual responsibility for acts and omissions. Republicans will remain focussed on broadsweep, movement- based commemorations that work to ethnicize and nationalize the public realm. This post-hoc and structuralist agenda will continue to resonate with sections of the human rights lobby, victims sector, civil society and academia. These points are deduced from the view that Irish nationalism is as unified as at any time in the recent past[1] and is as maximizing as at any time since the first half of the 1990s or even the period following internment in 1971: But what this means is that there is no restraint, no forbearance on which to build common ground. Nationalism is not simply explorative or pushing for-

---

[1] See, for instance, Jocelyn Evans and Jonathan Tonge, 'Catholic, Irish and Nationalist: Evaluating the Importance of Ethno-National and Ethno-Religious Variables in Determining Nationalist Political Allegiance in Northern Ireland, *Nations and Nationalism*, 19 (2), 2013, pp. 357-75.

ward cultural demands – it is exploitative. The banking metaphor is apt: nationalism is about accruing concessions and accumulating political capital. Setbacks can be tolerated but gains are banked and further movement is plotted. I argue that the debate over legislating for the legacy of the Troubles[2] works to engender and cultivate those dynamics in that it is deeply saturated with unspoken ideological and political assumptions.[3]

Nationalism and the Past: Exploitation and Accumulation

When, in 2014, Gerry Adams spoke of using equality demands as a 'Trojan horse' as being central to the 'entire republican strategy' (to 'actually break these bastards') he was simply reaffirming a long-standing Sinn Féin policy.[4] In fact, as papers deposited by Tom Hartley in the Linen Hall Library suggest, that strategy can be dated to as far back as 1988. At an internal party conference that year Hartley argued that the SDLP's 'green wing' was vulnerable and that 'every effort should be made by republicans to get the SDLP to take on board correct demands'. 'Correct demands', he went on to explain, 'do not necessarily have to be republican political demands, though it would be left to Sinn Féin to formulate such demands'. The point was that '[e]ach

---

[2] I tend towards the term 'Troubles' recognizing ethical objections to cognate nouns such as 'conflict' or 'war', which imply some kind of a justifiable basis for the violence that occurred in Northern Ireland. However, in an effort to avoid repetitions as far as possible I also deploy 'conflict'.

[3] See Cillian McGrattan, '"Order out of chaos": The Politics of Transitional Justice'. *Politics*, 29 (3), 2009, pp. 164-72.

[4] Quoted in Pete Baker '"that's the Trojan horse of the entire republican strategy..."', *Slugger O'Toole*, 25 November 2014.

time the SDLP move into a position of accepting as its policy one of these demands Sinn Féin should proceed to up the ante by bringing forward new demands'. At that same conference the Máirtín Ó Muilleoir supported this strategy of outflanking. For instance, he suggested that even if Sinn Féin tackled what he called 'mainstream' political issues such as NHS cutbacks, then 'we will be seen as having an intelligent and vigorous response to the political issue which affects our people and our hospitals ... The possibilities are endless, but [taking the initiative] will undoubtedly help boost our credibility, strengthen our base and entrench us in the political mainstream'.

The arguments deployed in 1988 speak to a political culture that revolves around a seeming paradox of shameless self-reflexivity. For, as Ó Muilleoir went on to explain, despite the 'contradictions between the armed struggle and our political work' – ostensibly the fact that the IRA was shooting workers and blowing up workplaces – republicans should 'not beat ourselves up about them ... At the very least', he concluded, 'let's be mature enough to discuss the contradictions'.[5] The idea of shameless self-reflexivity might be seen as akin to the ethic of 'survive and profit' and is, I would suggest, something intrinsic and deeply embedded in the republican worldview. It is not simply comparable to the shark metaphor deployed by the Irish diplomat Seán Ó Uiginn to describe Irish nationalism (namely that it requires perpetual momentum: '[i]t must keep moving or it dies'[6]) because it is not simply explorative but rather is fundamentally exploitative

[5] Quotations taken from Cillian McGrattan, *Northern Ireland, 1968-2008: The Politics of Entrenchment* (Basingstoke: Palgrave Macmillan, 2010), pp.129-30.
[6] Eamon Delaney, *An Accidental Diplomat: My Years in the Irish Foreign Service, 1987-1995* (Dublin: New Island, 2001), p. 305.

– hence the argument for the banking metaphor: republicans accrue concessions and accumulate political capital.

Transitional justice is an appealing market for this strategy because its fundamentally a priori methodology as relating to the past mirrors the structuralist logic of republicans that '[t]hey never went looking for war, but it came to them'.[7] Transitional justice in Northern Ireland has facilitated republicans turning what ought to have been a hostile environment (namely, the historical record of over 2,000 attributable deaths, almost 60 percent of the total murder count, in a sectarian campaign of assassination and bombings – not to mention the accompanying litany of bloodshed, unblinking cruelty and lives destroyed) into a fertile soil – in the process, allowing them to sustain a campaign of commemoration on 'an industrial scale'.[8] The political culture of transitional justice does not jar with its post-hoc methodology and has proven attractive to academia and 'community' organizations with the core aims of the approach having saturated thinking about the past to such an extent that it is questionable whether it is an overstatement to suggest that they enjoy a normative consensus.

The critical point in all this is that this is not simply a case of contemporary concerns reading-back into the past – a playing out of the kind of memory or cultural wars that seemingly inevitably follow any change in the political environment (whether it is a movement from authoritarianism to democracy or civil

---

[7] Michelle O'Neill cited in Adrian Rutherford, 'Watch: Sinn Féin leader Michelle O'Neill attends vigil for four IRA men killed by SAS', *Belfast Telegraph*, 16 February 2017.

[8] Henry McDonald, *Gunsmoke and Mirrors: How Sinn Féin Dressed Up Defeat as Victory* (Dublin: Gill & Macmillan, 2008), p. 121.

war to peace).[9] Nor is it simply about transmitting historical and moral relativism to future generations. Instead, the key argument of this paper is that the saturation of the republican and transitional justice methodology and approach to the past within policy design is almost complete: It is evidenced in the epigraph to the Eames/Bradley Consultative Group on the Past Report to the effect that the proper use of the past is to refresh our gaze in looking to the future; and it is evidenced in Richard Haass's reported comment that history is comparable to a Rorschach Blot – that we read into it what we like. My core argument is that this saturation means that there is no possible ground on which to speak clearly and evidentially about the past and what took place in Northern Ireland during the Troubles. It is not the case that the landscape has become polarized as this infers two or more strongholds; instead, the landscape has become ideologized – or republicanized – to such an extent that it is barely possible to imagine rational discussions about a whole host of issues related to the violence that claimed almost 4,000 deaths.

Transitional Justice – A Harmful Homeopathy

'Transitional justice' remains a disputed term – the idea of 'transition', for example, can be seen to denote a politically directed movement and its linking to 'justice' might be seen to give way to an 'altered – and lesser – form of justice', a form linked to a particular historical moment.[10] The International Center

---

[9] See Elizabeth Jelin, *State Repression and the Labors of Memory*. Trans. Judy Rein and Marcial Godoy-Anativia. (Minneapolis, University of Minnesota Press 2003).

[10] Tricia D. Olsen, Leigh A. Payne, and Andrew G. Reiter, *Transitional Justice in Balance: Comparing Processes, Weight Efficacy* (Washington: United States Institute for Peace, 2010), p. 10.

for Transitional Justice (ICTJ) offers a catch-all definition that stresses the importance of rules, roles and procedures: Transitional justice 'measures', it avers, 'include criminal prosecutions, truth commissions, reparations programs and various kinds of institutional reforms. Transitional justice, the Center states, 'is not a "special" kind of justice', it is, rather, 'an approach to achieving justice in times of transition from conflict and/or state repression'. The objective, it goes on to claim is that by 'trying to achieve accountability and redressing victims, transitional justice provides recognition of the rights of victims, promotes civic trust and strengthens the democratic rule of law'.[11]

- The transitional justice *approach* to peace-building is essentially structuralist and statist in orientation. That is to say, it broadly looks to patterns of causation it has emerged from a concern with instances of regime change in Latin America – as a result, the focus has tended towards crimes perpetrated by authoritarian regimes. Of course, these tendencies can be traced to the fact that transitional justice takes its *raison d'être* from the Nuremburg trials after the Second World War and is seen to encompass a range of judicial mechanisms such as the International Criminal Tribunal for the Former Yugoslavia (ICTY) and quasi-judicial institutions based on storytelling and emphasising restorative justice such as the South African Truth and Reconciliation Commission. Even with the proviso that the genealogy of transitional justice is associated with regime change rather than peace-building its the record is patchy: the example of the Tokyo tribunal is largely forgotten while

---

[11] International Centre for Transitional Justice [ICTJ], 'What is transitional justice?' Available at http://ictj.org/about/transitional-justice.

'[t]he long and exhaustive process of confrontation of the Nazi past in Germany is better traced as beginning from the activation of domestic judicial institutions in the 1960s than to a military tribunal founded by occupying powers in the 1940s'.[12] The structuralist and state-directed bias is made clear in the ICTJ's description of the *activities* of transitional justice: 'Because systemic human rights violations affect not just the direct victims, but society as a whole' the organization argues 'states have duties to guarantee that the violations will not recur, and therefore, a special duty to reform institutions that were either involved in or incapable of preventing the abuses'. The organization's description of its objectives goes on to contend that a 'history of unaddressed massive abuses is likely to be socially divisive, to generate mistrust between groups and in the institutions of the State [*sic*], and to hamper or slow down the achievement of security and development goals'[13]

• The _methodology_ of transitional justice is post-hoc and a priori: Beginning with an assumption of transition (a Year Zero typically where an authoritarian, anti-democratic regime collapses), it looks to deepen democratization efforts by uncovering historic injustices and oppressions. The basic idea is that securing justice through the recovery of truth(s) about past crimes and bringing

---

[12] Gordy, *Guilt*, p. 169; see also John Dower's conclusion that in regard to Tokyo Tribunal, '[s]o substantial … [were the] omissions that it does not seem too harsh to speak of criminal neglect, or even collusion, on the part of the prosecution itself'; John Dower, *Ways of Forgetting, Ways of Remembering: Japan in the Modern World* (New York: The New Press, 2012), p. 124.

[13] ICTJ, 'What is transitional justice'.

perpetrators to book will facilitate democratization by encouraging openness, accountability and transparency ('commitment to the rule of law') in post-conflict and post-authoritarian societies. Where political considerations are taken into account in this type of analysis they relate to the contestation between different versions of history or 'the truth'. The harnessing of justice to truth displaces questions of social responsibility for traumatized victims and confines societal transition within the framework of institutions and procedures. For example, in what has become one of the seminal works in contemporary transitional justice, Ruti Teitel, asks what happens when the shared understandings on which a polity (she argues) is based shatter.[14] Her objective is 'to resituate the rule-of-law dilemma by exploring societal experiences that arise in the context of political transformation ... [and] to attempt to understand the meaning of the rule of law for societies undergoing massive political change'.[15] As Omar Encarnación has demonstrated, the Spanish transition occurred despite rather than because of the overarching goal of transitional justice for reconciliation-through-historical confrontation. He points out that an under-appreciated unintended consequence of transitional justice is the danger that it 'morphs' into what he calls 'transitional revenge', leading to the deconsolidation of democratic achievements.[16]

---

[14] Ruti G. Teitel, *Transitional Justice* (Oxford: Oxford University Press, 2000), p. 6.

[15] *Ibid* p. 12.

[16] Omar G. Encarnación, *Democracy without Justice in Spain: The Politics of Forgetting* (Philadelphia, PA: The University of Pennsylvania Press, 2014).

- The voidance of shared meaning is equated with the
need to cultivate consensus and the juridical process
is held to be the key mechanism of transition: 'It is
through the framework of law, the language, procedures and vocabulary of justice, that ... reconstruction
is advanced'.[17] Following from this, democratization
must be seen to consist of the restoration of stability.
The _prescription_ is curiously homeopathic: the rationale
seems to be that 'like cures like' – in other words, because violence is the result of the absence of 'The Law',
then peace must be fostered with the creation of justice.
For example, Teitel argues that '[transitions] are periods
when shared notions of political truth and history are
largely absent', she claims; '[i]n transition, the very foci
of shared judgement that form the basis for a new social
consensus are expected to emerge through the historical
accountings'.[18]. However, the political nuances involved
in such issues are easily set aside in what is an essentially
legalistic understanding of political transition in which
History exists to underpin The Law. Thus, for Teitel:
'What makes for transitional accountability is generated
by forms and practices within a legal system. Transitional histories reveal how certain legal forms and practices
enable historical productions enable historical productions and transformed truths, shedding new light on
our intuitions about the role of history in liberalising
political change. Collective memory is created in frameworks and through symbols and rituals. In transition,
the oft-shared frameworks – political, religious, and social – are threatened; so it is the law, its framework, and

---

[17] Teitel, *Transitional Justice*, p. 72.
[18] *Ibid* p. 71.

processes that in great part shape collective memory. In transitions, the pivotal role in shaping social memory is played by the law.[19]

Shared Ventures: Transitional Justice and Northern Irish Republicanism

Although the British state accounted for around 10 percent of the total number of conflict-related fatalities in comparison with the 58.8 percent attributable to the PIRA and other republican terrorist groups,[20] in Sinn Féin's view 'The British state was the major protagonist in the conflict'. This conclusion arises from its narrative understanding of Irish history, which proceeds from the idea that 'British policy in Ireland is at the root of cyclical conflict here'.[21] The party's recommendations reflect this viewpoint, but also incorporate insights from the broader truth recovery paradigm. As with transitional justice, the _approach_ is statist and structural:

> What is needed is a truth-recovery mechanism which will help: [t]o make known the truth about the conflict; [t]o take seriously the needs of all victims; [t]o build in society the capacity to distinguish the truth from the myths; [t]o learn lessons about the past in order to guard against future conflict; [t]o broaden ownership of and responsibility for the process of conflict transformation; [and t]o explore conditions under which political actors can nurture greater trust, confidence, and generosity towards each other.[22]

---

[19] *Ibid* p. 71.

[20] McKittrick *et al*, *Lost Lives*, p. 1482.

[21] Sinn Féin 'Truth recovery', p. 12. Author copy.

[22] *Ibid* p. 28.

The idea that Irish history is cyclical and determined by the injustice perpetuated by British state involvement is, of course, not restricted to Sinn Féin.[23] However, the narrative of British culpability does reflect a specifically totalising or systemic understanding of the conflict that characterises Provisional republicanism, particularly the political use of the narrative to advance the claim that the conflict was essentially structural and that truth recovery should not dwell on individual culpability. The *methodology* then works to uncover 'causes' of that diagnosis. This idea is encapsulated in a report by the Eolas network, which coordinated 'grassroots' initiatives in Belfast:

> Our justice is generally one of looking at the systemic nature, causes and extent of the conflict, examining the nature of the system that allowed and facilitated actions as opposed to the person or people who carried out these actions.[24]

In pointing out the complicity of the British state in 'systemic' human rights abuses, the Eolas document effectively precludes the idea that any truth recovery process could be run by the British government. This idea is echoed by other republican-oriented victims groups such as Relatives for Justice and the Pat Finucane Centre:

---

[23] See, for example, the key SDLP position paper, which formed the basis of the party's approach to the peace negotiations of the 1990s, "SDLP analysis of the nature of the problem: submission to Brooke Talks, June 1991", Linen Hall Library, Northern Ireland Political Collection, P9283.

[24] Eolas, 'Consultation Paper on Truth and Justice' (2003), Available at http://healingthroughremembering.info/images/j_library/lib/Eolas.pdf.

> It is the considered view of our organisations that an inde-
> pendent, international truth commission is the mechanism
> of truth recovery that would benefit the greatest number
> of families who have been bereaved through the conflict.[25]

The Provisional republican approach to dealing with the past
draws sustenance and inspiration from academic connections.
These tend to coincide with a common understanding over
prognoses: namely, a belief in (and a framing of) the utility of
transitional justice (and, relatedly, community-based restorative
justice) in Northern Ireland.[26] Often, this is a result of academics
linked with transitional justice in the two universities directly
advising community groups. For example, Brandon Hamber of
Ulster University 'facilitated' the Eolas Consultative Paper, while
two other UU sociologists, Bill Rolston and Patricia Lundy, were
also involved in the project.[27] This community and academic
work tends to promote the idea that truth recovery is necessary
to build peace and achieve reconciliation:

> For advocates of truth recovery, dealing with the past and
> uncovering the truth is regarded as a key cornerstone and
> basis upon which trust can begin to be built and society
> can move forward.[28]

---

[25] The Pat Finucane Centre, 'Open Letter from Justice for the Forgotten, the Pat Finucane Centre and Relatives for Justice, 2 July 2007'.
Available from: http://www.serve.com/pfc/truth/ol_panel.html.

[26] Cillian McGrattan 'Community-Based Restorative Justice in
Northern Ireland: A Neo-Traditionalist Paradigm?' *British Journal of
Politics and International Relations*, 2010, Vol. 12 (3): 408-424.

[27] See http://www.brandonhamber.com/clients.htm; see also Eolas,
'Consultation', p. 2.

[28] Patricia Lundy and Mark McGovern, 'Attitudes towards a Truth
Commission for Northern Ireland in Relation to Party Political

Reasonable and laudable as the ideals of building trust and moving forward are, they are also nevertheless structurally biased.[29] This is revealed in their intensely political framing of the debate in Northern Ireland in which concern for due process and the punishment of terrorist and state crimes or ideas about historical accuracy, are downplayed or ignored in favour of an over-determined dichotomy between 'restorative' and 'retributive conception[s] of justice'.[30] While Lundy and her one-time co-author Mark McGovern attempt to engage unionism in substantive debate,[31] this perceived broadening simply ignores the possibility that unionism does not necessarily wish to engage in and on the terms of the transitional and progressivist paradigm. For example, the most comprehensive account of unionist politics since the 1998 Agreement and – in particular – unionists' attitudes towards the post-conflict situation points out that 'unionists *want to tell their stories*, but fear that in [so] doing they will subject those stories to critical scrutiny, and that they will potentially become inadvertent participants in truth projects that will elide their histories of suffering'.[32] Lundy and McGovern co-edited the Ardoyne Commemoration Project's storytelling initiative

---

Affiliation', *Irish Political Studies*, 22 (3), (2007), p. 323.

[29] Henry Patterson, 'Truth and Reconciliation in Northern Ireland? Not Much Hope of Either', *Parliamentary Brief*, February, 2009.

[30] Patricia Lundy and Mark McGovern, 'Attitudes towards a Truth Commission in Northern Ireland', *Irish Political Studies*, 22 (3), 2007, p. 321-22.

[31] Patricia Lundy and Mark McGovern, 'A Trojan Horse? Unionism, Trust and Truth-telling in Northern Ireland', *The International Journal of Transitional Justice*, 2 (1), pp. 42-62.

[32] Simpson, *Unionist Voices and the Politics of Remembering the Past in Northern Ireland* (Basingstoke: Palgrave Macmillan, 2009), p. 122; original emphasis.

Ardoyne: The Untold Truth.[33] Although the group's rationale was to recount the stories of the 99 people who died in the community during the Troubles, an insight into Lundy and McGovern's methodology is contained in the fact that the book makes only a passing reference to the killing of the 'at least a dozen civilians from unionist areas ... that lie within or are immediately adjacent to Ardoyne' – not to mention the state 'combatants'. At the risk of labouring the political and ethical implications of that methodology: The selectivity raises the profile of one category of victims while effectively silencing others.

The progressivist commitment to a 'holistic, community-oriented approach' misses this point: it is wishful thinking to suppose that such an approach may 'open up' 'spaces of controversy' (or, in Sinn Féin's verbiage, 'uncomfortable conversations') and 'allow testimony to be translated into an exchange of trust'[34] when the overriding fear of unionists is that 'imposed, manufactured history by Irish republicans (with assistance from the British and/or Irish governments) would elide' individual and collective 'biographies of suffering'.[35] Furthermore, the structural bias of the progressivist approach recurs in the complaint that '[s]ome of the strongest opposition to truth recovery has come from within unionism and loyalism'.[36] This is in fact a common nationalist trope in which a community that repudiated violence and espoused democratic means of resolving the conflict is coupled with terrorists. Loyalist spokespersons have, unsurprisingly, adopted the same self-serving, self-exculpatory approach of

---

[33] Ardoyne Commemoration Project, *Ardoyne: The Untold Truth* (Belfast: Beyond the Pale, 2002).

[34] Lundy and McGovern, 'A Trojan Horse', p. 62.

[35] Simpson, *Unionist Voices*, p. 115.

[36] Lundy and McGovern, 'Attitudes', p. 323.

Provisional republicans[37] Lundy and McGovern's obliviousness to this dynamic reveals not only the limitations of the progressivist paradigm but also its potential for coinciding with ethno national viewpoints. For example, the implications of the 'holistic, community-oriented approach' are similar to those that emanate from the loyalist compliant about being ostracized from mainstream unionism as a result of their campaign of sectarian violence.[38]

Amnesty and Transitional Justice

Transitional justice may cause more hurt, damage and contention than it smooths; homeopathic in purpose it is less similar to a placebo than it is to a nocebo – the effect of a sham treatment inducing a worsening of symptoms or the nullification of analgesic or anaesthetics. The transitional metaphor is replete with homeopathic-esque promises: restoration, reconciliation and truth recovery. The problem is that it is not just only very hard to argue against these terms without seeming arbitrarily hostile or curmudgeonly, it is that the framing of those terms by transitional justice advocates and theorists ushers-in unspoken assumptions about the politics of the past and the methods of approaching it. The transitional justice model of peace-building, then, is saturated with ethical and political import, its success is because not despite these problems because it remains a proceduralist paradigm: Dividing the past from the present also means parcelling out societal memories about that past, siphoning some off for special treatment and discarding or marginalizing those it deems unsatisfactory. This is exemplified in the transitional justice approach to amnesty – driven in Northern

---

[37] McGrattan, '"Order"'

[38] EPIC *Truth Recovery: A Contribution from Loyalism* (Belfast: EPIC, 2004).

Ireland by Professors Brandon Hamber and Louise Mallinder of Ulster University and Professor Kieran McEvoy of Queen's.[39]

The precedent seems to be the South African model of a truth recovery process that offers amnesties in return for truth. Mark Osiel, for instance, has suggested that when accompanied with a range of obligations that tie new regimes and leaders to human rights protocols, amnesty processes can provide for some level of the truth about crimes being achieved. But, he argues, amnesty often fails when it is not accompanied by a 'power transfer to new leaders who are genuinely committed to human rights'.[40] The point seems to be that amnesty serves power interests and foster a *carte blanche* attitude to violent pasts that inevitably bolsters the interests of perpetrators over their victims. This was, roughly, the approach of the South African Truth and Reconciliation Commission (TRC). As Mahmood Mamdani pointed out, the South African transition was planned before the TRC was set up and that amnesty was promised to perpetrators

> not in exchange for truth-telling but, crucially, for joining the process of political reform. The negotiations were conducted with the aim of ending political and juridical apartheid. They involved inevitable compromises on both sides, without which the transition could not have been achieved.[41]

---

[39] https://www.ulster.ac.uk/__data/assets/pdf_file/0005/57839/The-BelfastGuidelinesFINAL_000.pdf; revealingly, academic freedom of thought seems to have been placed on hiatus during the composition of the report: 'It was agreed at the outset that no member should be entitled to enter a personal dissent or reservation' (p. 4).

[40] Mark Osiel, *Making Sense of Mass Atrocity* (Cambridge: Cambridge University Press, 2009), p. 224.

[41] Mahmood Mamdani, 'The Logic of Nuremburg', *The London*

As such, amnesty incorporates substantive issues concerning ethical principles and long-term, transgenerational judgments. These issues lie at the heart of the French philosopher Paul Ricoeur's alternative and critical views of amnesty, which he defined as 'organized forgetting'. Ricoeur claimed that they 'do wrong at once to truth, thereby repressed and as if forbidden, and to justice, at it is due to the victims';[42] instead, he advocated a historically and empirically informed approach in which critical history becomes married with a sense of justice.[43]

Despite a claim of being guided by 'an Expert Group of internationally respected human rights and conflict resolution scholars and practitioners',[44] Mallinder *et al* do not engage with Ricoeur's work (or indeed any sustained or serious counter-arguments). The report proposes that amnesties should be considered to assist transitions and conflict transformation. However, as with the contextual selectivity of Lundy and McGovern, Mallinder *et al's* methodology involves a kind of telescoping – this time, sequencing is abridged. For, to take seriously Osiel's point about commitments to rights and norms, then one ought really to consider the counterfactual of what happens if amnesties are implemented in the absence of this commitment, before, that is, promoting the policy. This seems, in my reading, the circle that the DUP's amnesty proposals are trying to square. Linked with

---

Review of Books, 35 (21), 7 November 2013, pp. 34.

[42] Paul Ricoeur and Sorin Antohi, 'Memory, History, Forgiveness: A Dialogue between Paul Ricoeur and Sorin Antohi'. Available at http://www.janushead.org/8-1/ricoeur.pdf.

[43] See Paul Ricoeur, *Memory, History, Forgetting* (Chicago: University of Chicago Press, 2004).

[44] https://www.ulster.ac.uk/__data/assets/pdf_file/0005/57839/The-BelfastGuidelinesFINAL_000.pdf

the idea of a commitment to general, liberal democratic norms, the idea of culpability is mentioned only once in a report that makes much play of accountability is initially perplexing. But the political effect of downplaying or displacing culpability is to work to dissociate responsibility from accountability. In this way, judgment is deferred in favour of an explanation of choices: in other words, perpetrators of crimes are required to justify and explain their actions but will not be held culpable.

It is difficult to take seriously Mallinder's claim that she and her colleagues 'look at international best practice' when unpalatable evidence or inconvenient cases are ignored.[45] A similar accusation can be levelled at the Northern Ireland Human Rights' Commission's advocacy of transitional justice.[46] Mallinder's assertion was made to the Committee for the Administration of Justice in regards to the proposed Independent Commission on Information Retrieval (ICIR), which was designed as a non-prosecutorial complement to the police-driven Historical Investigations Unit. She went on to pinpoint a key lacuna in the ICIR relating to the lack of disincentives for disclosing information to the body. But, rather bizarrely, she asserts that 'there should be penalties for people who provide false information ... or people who otherwise obstruct the commission's work perhaps by destroying documents'. Bizarrely, because this is the whole point of the ICIR. However, her argument is surreptitiously politically loaded to undermine the investigatory body by beefing-up the truth recovery one. Her point about sequencing is also moot – Mallinder, for instance, argues that ICIR cases would be put on hold un-

---

[45] https://caj.org.uk/2015/04/17/dealing-past-implementing-sha-conference-report-papers/

[46] http://www.nihrc.org/uploads/publications/NIHRC_Transitional_Justice_Report.pdf

til the HIU has finished. In the projected five-year period, this would mean, she asserts, the ICIR remaining dormant for most of the time. The obverse seems to be more immediately possible: namely, that terrorists would opt to place (non-admissible) testimony in the ICIR to effect immunity for themselves and their former colleagues. Of course, this point is almost entirely hypothetical as republicans have form with non-cooperation with judicial inquiries in the UK and the Republic.

It is *almost* hypothetical if it were not for the commitment in Haass/O'Sullivan and the Stormont House Agreement for proportionality. Unfortunately, for transitional justice advocates this term does not actually seem to apply to the historical record, but rather in the procedures applied to the past. So, Anna Bryson argues that proportionality is needed in 'deciding [what material] can be made public and ... [what] should be withheld'.[47] The methodology remains vague but targeted – we are unsure as to how such decisions will or even if they can be made, but we are certain that they need to be, seems to be the message. The certainty comes from the apparent belief that something must be done and therein lies the ideology of transitional justice – strategy slides into categorical imperatives and issues of practicality and ethics are paid lip service in the knowledge that when delivery of service goes wrong none is going to go back to the documents to check for the origins of the initiatives. If the point is to be always transitioning, then a rationale does not really need to be spelled out.

Although storytelling remains an invaluable tool for countering oblivion of memory, it is also an analgesic treatment that engenders the type of amnesia feared by Ricoeur. In political terms, it can work as a loaded dice and seems to particularly lends itself to romanticized notions about the past.

---

[47] *Ibid.*

Conclusions

Amnesty is, in any case, something of a red herring politically and socially speaking. The Belfast/Good Friday Agreement provided a *de facto* amnesty in any case and militates against former terrorists offering South African-style 'full disclosures' in return for testimony in case they place their or a colleague's impunity at risk. In this regard the DUP proposal for guillotine legislation in relation to service personnel seems more like exasperation at the tilted playing field than an attempt to redress the balance of play. The idea of amnesty is also moot because the rewriting of history as and through commemoration continues apace, particularly, within northern nationalism. Indeed, I have sought to convey the argument that the politics of dealing with the past are now so skewered that any attempt to redefine the rules of the game will be futile.

As part of the Arkiv group, based within social sciences at Ulster University but drawing on the expertise and resources of colleagues from across the UK, I have argued for historical clarification as a means of hedging off an area of knowledge and judgment about the past based on the empirical and archival evidence. We suggested that even if republicans and loyalists would not cooperate that knowledge is still largely accessible based on archival source material. For the past decade or so, for instance, political historians have been using state papers available under the thirty- and twenty-year rules to deconstruct anti-revisionist and traditional nationalist interpretations of key events of the Troubles (including its origins, the civil rights movement, Sunningdale, the hunger strikes, the Anglo-Irish Agreement) and its overall trajectory. We suggested that such an instrument would be necessary to counter-act the 'Google-ization' of memory through the archiving of stories.[48] The EU-funded, Accounts of the Conflict, which is housed at Ulster University for instance, (at the time of writing, February 2018) contains no information on Bloody Friday or the Falls Road Curfew.[49] Arkiv argued that a historically informed account of the conflict would at least help to reduce the range of 'permissible lies' that could be told.

Republicans seem to have decided that their objective in entering into those politics is to forward the transitional arrangements of the 1998 environment. I have argued that reconciliation on those terms is a myth. Although I have concentrated on republicans and academics, the SDLP has ghosted the paper simply because republicans' aggressive, sustained and systemic exploitation of the past would not be possible if it were not tacitly and overtly facilitated by the 'moderate' nationalist party. In reality, the SDLP provides a gloss of respectability for republicans' ultra-ethnic approach to dealing with the past; but scratch at the gloss and it quickly peels off: witness the McCreesh playpark fiasco, the paper thin distinctions between the policy papers of the two parties, the commitment of key spokespersons to the republican narrative of systemic collusion – it is difficult, for example, to imagine either Hume or Mallon, for all their reactionary nationalist tendencies, carrying the coffin of a former terrorist.[50] That the SDLP is a party in the midst of collapse only

---

[48]   Cillian McGrattan, 'The Stormont House Agreement and the New Politics of Storytelling in Northern Ireland, *Parliamentary Affairs*, 4 (1), 2016, pp. 928-46.

[49]   http://accounts.ulster.ac.uk/repo24/index.php

[50]   *Belfast Telegraph*, 23 February 2016, 'SDLP chief Colum Eastwood has no regrets over carrying coffin of INLA man Seamus "Chang" Coyle'; at https://www.belfasttelegraph.co.uk/news/northern-ireland/sdlp-chief-colum-eastwood-has-no-regrets-over-carrying-coffin-of-in-la-man-seamus-chang-coyle-34477794.html.

compounds the problem: party affiliation/identification and ideology seem to ever more closely correlate within the nationalist bloc – a dynamic that seems set to continue given the radicalization of younger nationalist voters coming 'on stream'. (The Irish government's foot-dragging over legacy requests by victims and survivors and the PSNI and the seeming commitment of the Varadakar administration to escalate Brexit-related issues is only more evidence of that trend.)

Given this radicalization of nationalist politics, unionists are faced with a choice: To try to impose terms on the legacy legislation or to try to salvage something from the process. The risk is that by trying to do both unionists will come away with neither. This paper has tried to suggest that the concession-based approach of Sinn Féin and nationalism, aided and abetted by a transitional justice narrative and methodology, is deep rooted and advanced. The key difference, as I see it, between the desire to republicanize the 'mainstream' that interested Ó Muilleoir and Hartley in the 1980s is that that has largely occurred – certainly, in relation to the legacy debate. As a result, the mainstream no longer exists as a shared collection of common norms and understandings of decency, respect and restraint. I see nothing in the recent history of republicanism or the Northern Irish transitional justice sector to support a reading of tolerance or restraint; if anything, a maximalist agenda has been prepared and is being targeted. If this reading is plausible then unionists need to recognize that nationalists will not exercise restraint – the process can be neither controlled nor salvaged.

About the author

Cillian McGrattan lectures in politics at Ulster University. He is the author of a number of books on Northern Ireland: *Northern Ireland, 1968-2008: The Politics of Entrenchment* (Palgrave

Macmillan 2010); *The Northern Ireland Conflict* (Oneworld, 2010/12) (co-authored with Aaron Edwards); *Everyday Life after the Irish Conflict: The Impact of Devolution and North-South Cooperation* (Manchester University Press, 2012) (co-edited with Elizabeth Meehan); *Memory, Politics and Identity: Haunted by History* (Palgrave Macmillan, 2012); *The Politics of Trauma and Peacebuilding: Lessons from Northern Ireland* (Routledge, 2016/17); *Sunningdale and the Ulster Workers' Council Strike: The Struggle for Democracy in Northern* Ireland (Manchester University Press, 2017) (co-edited with David McCann).

Cillian McGrattan

The Past Being the Future

Andrew Charles

"The old has passed away; behold, the new has come."
2 Corinthians 5:17b

This year, on 10 April 2018, is the twentieth anniversary of the Belfast Agreement. To many, at the time, and still even today, especially many of whom live outside of Northern Ireland, this agreement was marked as being 'out with the old and in with the new'.

The Agreement is commonly referred to as the Good Friday Agreement, a reference to it being the subject of divine intervention. The Apostle Paul in 2 Corinthians 5:17b wrote: "The old has passed away; behold, the new has come." This, however has not been the Northern Ireland experience, albeit I acknowledge that the Apostle Paul referred to higher things.

In this paper, entitled 'The Past Being the Future', I wish to address a number of issues, namely:

- How we got here;
- How 'we' remain in a 'state of war'; and
- How and why we remain in such a place?

How we got here

The 1985 Anglo-Irish Agreement

It saw the London Government officially recognise the Government of the Republic of Ireland as having a say in the affairs of Northern Ireland after many years of viewing the Northern Ireland 'Troubles' as a domestic affair.

The Irish saw this as a major step forward, after all Article 2 and 3, which lay claim to the territory of Northern Ireland, remained in force. While, London, saw this as an arrangement for better security, mainly that of co-operation in respect of securing the arrest and questioning of 'Wanted' IRA Terrorists. This has been confirmed in Official Cabinet papers released under the thirty-year rule.

However, most relevant, and important for the purposes of this paper, London, or Britain, officially recognised an 'Irish' dimension to 'the problem'. It basically became 'identity' focused. Tactics changed from one of securitisation, or Ulsterisation, to the recognition of 'two traditions'.

Ulster University Speech by the Secretary of State Sir Patrick Mayhew, Coleraine, December 1992

The speech made by the Secretary of State was significant in retrospect. This was made clear in a paper presented by academic Richard English in *The Irish Review* (1994) where he argued:

In Northern Ireland, where insecurity, ambiguity, and uncertainty continue to have fatally destructive and destabilising consequences, such an incoherent approach granting equal legitimacy to opposing sets of cultural/political loyalties - seems to me to be deeply unhelpful.

English went onto argue that by the Government granting equal status to the Irish identity, including political aspirations, that it risked inflaming loyalist attitudes by granting legitimacy to the arguments for British withdrawal (1994; 100). For English this position only worked to heighten and enhance those insecurities and fears ever present within the Unionist community. English suggested that the position taken by HM Government handed loyalist paramilitaries momentum in delivering upon their aims and objectives through violence (1994; 100).

Arguably, English wrote and published this article before the Belfast Agreement, which had elite buy-in from loyalist paramilitaries represented at the talks table by the Progressive Unionist Party (PUP) and now defunct Ulster Democratic Party (UDP). Nevertheless, The Downing Street Declaration, had been published, much to the shock and surprise of Unionists. The London Government had also been engaged in 'talks' with the leadership of the Provisional IRA.

The risks of such a two-tier framework, enhanced by the Belfast Agreement, provided a framework for the waging of a cultural war by Republicans'. Which we are witnessing being played out today in respect of an Irish language Act.

1998 Belfast Agreement

The Belfast Agreement set out the clear government policy of the 'Two Traditions' Model, through the formal recognition of Irish and Britishness – side-by-side. This, in my view, was, and is, wholly dangerous; the outworking of which we see today.

The Two Traditions Model was enshrined in law, through the NI Act 1998, and institutionalised sectarianism, namely a segregation of mindset. This is primarily evidenced through the designation of members as being Unionist, Nationalist, or Other.

It is also evidenced through the D'Hondt Mechanism, which is the means of forming an Executive decided by party strength and the appointment of the First and Deputy First Ministers, who are equal in all but name.

How 'we' remain in a 'state of war'

Carl von Clausewitz in his publication *On War* argued that 'Politics is war by other means'. In the case of Northern Ireland, I regard this to be wholly correct. This goes beyond identity, being linked to legacy, language and culture.

Legacy, or 'The Past', is being utilised by Provisional Sinn Fein as a means of justifying their 'war', linking it to the continuation of the NI Civil Rights Movement of the 1960s, the demands of which were met under a Unionist Government by 1972.

Recently, Alex Maskey, Sinn Fein MLA for West Belfast, in responding to SDLP Leader Colum Eastwood, who said: "We can't forget that it took the Civil Rights Association here to ensure that all people got full access to voting rights". Maskey responded: "Unfortunately it took more than the CRA to secure rights in the putrid little statelet NI."

A number of issues require clarity here, arising from the assumptions of both Eastwood and Maskey: Roman Catholics had the vote in all elections in Northern Ireland before 1968. Eastwood's comment assumes that Roman Catholics did not have voting rights.

What he is (probably) referring to is the local government franchise. It is uniformly accepted (wrongly) that Roman Catholics were not entitled to vote in local government elections, as opposed to Protestants. This is not the case. In fact the ratepayer limitations in respect of the entitlement to vote in local government elections impacted more significantly on working-class Protestants. (Only ratepayers and their spouses were entitled to vote, whether in owner-occupied houses or tenants in rented property.)

While the franchise was limited, as it was in the rest of the United Kingdom until reformed im 1948, working-class Protestants, given their larger numbers, were *less* likely to have a vote in local government elections when compared to Roman Catholics. In fact, of those not entitled to vote in local government elections, Protestants made up 60 per cent of the disenfranchised. The franchise was reformed here in 1968 twenty years later than England.

Thirdly, and rather importantly, Maskey in his response sought to justify the Provisional IRA terrorist campaign under the banner of Civil Rights, something Provisional Sinn Fein have been seeking to do so for a number of years in the aftermath of their electoral successes over the SDLP.

The interaction between both politicians demonstrates a lack of understanding of history, or a lack of a will to appreciate the facts.

In fact, the night before the March Assembly election last year, 2016, a prominent political commentator posted on social media a picture of a mural in Londonderry depicting the Civil Rights Movement, with the statement "Remember what we fought for".

A prominent Sinn Fein politician made what this commentator was alluding to on live radio, stating that Roman Catholic's did not have the vote prior to 1998. The politician was not challenged nor informed of the inaccuracy of this statement.

The reality is that Provisional Sinn Fein are seeking to re-write history, comparing their campaign of violence, or that of the Provisional IRA, to something similar to that of the ANC in South Africa or the PLO/Hamas in Israel/Palestine. Two examples I see no foundation for, by way of information.

How and why we remain in such a place?

Earlier I referred to the Two Traditions Model and the Belfast Agreement. These two, or one, being that of the Agreement, enshrined the foundations for a new theatre of war.

Firstly, the Two Traditions Model is Institutionalised through Strand One of the Belfast Agreement. Power-sharing, or Consociationalism, is a curse, and some twenty years later must be looked at again, otherwise Northern Ireland will not 'move forward'.

Secondly, we have the recognition of former prisoners, or Terrorists, as community gatekeepers, people who the Police and other Statutory Agencies, work through in order to resolve community-based problems.

Then we also have the aspect of the 'peace dividend', which is more or less 'hush' money. This totals millions, if not billions of pounds per annum, yet our hospitals and education system, the two corner stones of the post-war UK, struggle to make ends meet and deliver on their 'targets'. This impacts upon ordinary 'Joe' public, but they do not connect the two.

Legacy, or 'the past' has become a sticking point. The campaign, led by Provisional Sinn Fein, is one of justifying the actions of their military wing – the Provisional IRA, by embarrassing the UK Government and appealing to ordinary decent people, who would not be naturally Sinn Fein voters, or those who did not grow up during 'the Troubles', to see the Provisional IRA Campaign of murder and ethnic cleansing as being comparable to that of EOKA in Cyprus, or that of the PLO/Hamas in Israel/Palestine (neither of which I would justify).

Whether people take a view one way or the other, they will say 'one side was as bad as the other'. However, the news that 'Letters of Comfort' were issued in side-deals between Sinn Fein and the Labour Party, therefore side-lining the justice system, did have some impact within the wider community. Nonetheless, it does not fill Unionists, or any decent law-abiding citizen with confidence or trust in our Government.

The rewriting of history also goes beyond Legacy, which I know is the focus of today, but I cannot not avoid mentioning a recent report into the exodus of Protestants from the West Bank of Londonderry. Yesterday a news report, written by the Pat Finucane Centre, argued that the exodus of Protestants was multifaceted. The mass exodus of Protestants from the Cityside had nothing to do with terrorism or fear, instead it was down to jobs and social deprivation. Again, Ladies and Gentlemen, we have the rewriting of history.

The Two Traditions Model has eaten its way into Government policy, which is seen through approaches to community relations policy, housing, and education (the latter two which were arguably 'segregated' prior to the current political setup. Transitional, or 'Restorative' justice is another, one sided, narrow example as to how 'justice' is practiced here in Northern Ireland.

Way forward

The mythology of Protestants, or Unionists, standing firm under the phrase of 'No Surrender', seems to be what it is labelled, a myth.

The way forward however is to challenge these historical inaccuracies and to stand up and be counted. These issues threaten the very future of Northern Ireland, for example, what are our post-Agreement generations to believe?

It is up to us to lobby for change, call people out for historical accuracy, lobby for truth, and most importantly justice for victims of terrorism.

I think it is especially important to hear from all sections of civil society, especially our churches and numerous 'Unionist' groups as we must remember the words of one Robert Sands (if they were even his): "Our revenge will be the laughter of our children."

Andrew Charles

The Past: Drawing a Line?

Austen Morgan

Introduction

The past in Northern Ireland should not be in dispute, but it is. A new state was created, by Irish republicans, using political violence, in 1919-21, in about 30 months. In the 30 years from 1968 to 1998, Sinn Féin/the IRA, despite greater force, failed to annex its fourth green field[1] (the north): it, and Irish nationalism, secured the Belfast agreement (a name its ideologues cannot utter) and a secret so-called peace process.

It took far too long for the casualties of 'the troubles' to be recognized with the striking statistics (rounded up) on those killed over three decades: republicans being responsible for 60 per cent (including many catholics); loyalists for 30 per cent (including many protestants); and the state – police and soldiers – being responsible for approximately 10 per cent of all deaths, some 361.[2]

Any humanitarian would be concerned about the approximately 3,500 plus deaths, the very many more injured (often permanently), and of course the survivors and relatives. But there is a constitutional context, and in particular the distinction between being killed lawfully or unlawfully. That is where religion, and emotion, gives way to law, and to reason. The 90 per cent of paramilitary murders were unlawful: only some of the 10 per cent state killings – a handful – was unlawful.

---

[1] Tommy Makem, 'Four green fields' (1967).

[2] I first analyzed the statistics in 'Jordan and After: the right to life in Northern Ireland', published subsequently in my internet book, *The Hand of History?: legal essays on the Belfast Agreement* (London 2011), pp 144-87: available www.austenmorgan.com

This remains the position even when some attempt to argue, taking leave of the rule of law, that the principal perpetrator, the IRA, challenged a UK constitutional norm and created an Irish one, of greater legitimacy; thus, its idea of legitimate targets, the pursuit of which was mired in much blood and sectarianism.

So, why are we stuck in a post-troubles period (of now 20 years), characterized by: first, holding the state to account for its killings; and, secondly, effectively excusing republican, but not loyalist, paramilitaries for most of the illegality? The answer is culture, ideology and reasoning, fed by bad politics, and in particular the expediencies of the UK and Irish states.

We have 'the past' as an issue in NI, seemingly to be 'solved' by a set of more public bodies stuffed with quangocrats. And, on the other hand, we have 'transitional justice' well rooted in academic law in NI[3], prosecuting the state ideologically while exonerating republicans (the loyalists, through 'collusion', being agents of the state!).

I stunned myself when I first wrote that the Saville bloody Sunday report[4] would lead the rest of the world to have a somewhat distorted view of NI.[5] It does. I now wonder whether any NI lawyers ever told the Strasbourg human rights court – when arguing their article 2 cases (which applied originally to all survivors and relatives) – about the numbers 60/30/10. I suspect not. Strasbourg now treats the UK state as the principal offender, effectively helping republicans refight the troubles as propaganda in forums more congenial, and less dangerous, than the original ones: Loughgall (1987), Gibraltar (1988), Finucane (1989),

---

[3] The transitional justice institute in Ulster university (2003) and the school of law/senator George J. Mitchell institute for global peace, security and justice in Queen's University, Belfast.

[4] *Report of the Bloody Sunday Inquiry*, HC 29 2010-11, 15 June 2010.

[5] See n 2 above, p 148.

Loughinisland (1994).

I recently had the opportunity to reflect upon this weird situation, when, following John Downey walking free from the Old Bailey in February 2014 (due to English justice!), I used the papers from the case to write: *Tony Blair and the IRA: the 'on the runs' scandal* (London 2016). This book has been well received generally: but those in NI's two universities yet to comment upon the on the runs ('OTRs'), have somehow failed to join in this constitutional critique of Tony Blair.

In the conclusion to the book, which I draw upon in this paper, I discussed, in chapter 13, prosecution or amnesty? Conscious that I might be seen to be agitating for the prosecution of John Downey (in NI for the Hyde Park bombing?), I actually – on balance – came out in favour of a statutory amnesty for all. This was not to forget the past: it was to ensure it could be recorded more accurately, by the writing of good history and the cultural drawing of proper lessons. The Downey papers are only a small proportion of official archives in London, Belfast and Dublin. There is much more in warehouses and other locations.

I was influenced strongly in my decision by the scandal of the OTRs, and the fact that Whitehall – between 2000 and 2014 – had run an administrative scheme, through which 187 IRA members (no loyalists were included) of 228 applicants had benefited from a secret amnesty, before its sudden collapse due to John Downey's successful abuse of process application.

The OTR scandal, I believe, has inspired an alternative movement, of supporters of soldiers and police, calling for a statute of limitation on the prosecution of those responsible for NI's state killings.[6]

---

[6] Armed forces (statute of limitations) bill: HC Hansard, vol. 630, cols. 823-5, 1 November 2017. Second reading, 15 June 2018.

The Future: Prosecution or Amnesty?

What is the future for NI: either the prosecution of republican terrorists and others or an amnesty for all troubles crimes, committed between 1968 and 1998?

Having written the Tony Blair book, and reflected on this general question substantively for the first time, I surprised myself in arguing against the prosecution of the OTRs. However, I am only interested in the idea of a statutory amnesty, if it applies equally to everyone. The lessons of the Northern Ireland (Offences) bill of 2005-06, which Tony Blair failed to put through parliament, need to be learned. This has implications, of course, for the more recent movement, calling for a statute of limitations, to reassure the many police and soldiers who may feel at risk of prosecution.

My view is based upon a complex of reasons for and against, to do with each of the alternatives: prosecution or amnesty. It is not an easy debate to initiate. First, I weigh the case for prosecution. Then, I look at amnesty. And finally, I balance prosecution against amnesty, coming down eventually on one side.

Prosecution

The following are seven important arguments, for or against prosecution:

- one, the victims: 3,720 persons died violently, between 1966 and 2006 (and more since)[7], and very many more were injured, creating a huge (and growing) sector of victims and survivors[8]. Each victim deserves justice

---

[7] David McKittrick & Others, eds., *Lost Lives,* Edinburgh & London, 2007, p. 1553.

[8] Victims and Survivors (Northern Ireland) Order 2006, SI 2006/2953; Commission for Victims and Survivors Act (Northern Ireland) 2008.

without question, and varying groups of relatives and supporters have demanded variously, and increasingly, inquiries, inquests, investigations and prosecutions;

- two, the perpetrators: the figures for who killed whom are clear. If all unlawful killings were to be pursued equally, the investigations etc. would be overwhelmingly against republican and loyalist paramilitaries, including those who have now abandoned violence for politics;

- three, legacy litigation: this unfortunately goes with the grain of propaganda. The republicans divert attention from themselves as the principal culprits by focusing on state killings and construing loyalist murders incorrectly as collusion. The state has archives, and the government seeks to discharge its legal obligations by restricting disclosure. There are no such requirements imposed on republican and loyalist organizations. The impression is reinforced, by increasing calls for inquests, inquiries and investigations, that the troubles were really about a succession of direct and indirect state abuses which the IRA heroically resisted;

- four, humanitarian concerns for victims and survivors: grieving is a necessary emotional response to death and injury, and there is a growing need for private and public provision of services, therapeutic, medical and social. Few appear to have asked the macro question in this context: would more people begin to feel better more quickly, with a continuation of sectarian polarization (as has happened) or with genuine reconciliation promoted by the state (as has happened in other societies)?;

According to the victims and survivors service, an average of ten new victims comes forward each day: *Belfast Telegraph*, 30 October 2014.

- five, the concept of criminal justice: is it necessary to have open-ended historic investigations (and reparations) or, as most constitutional states do, have a statute of limitation for criminal liability?;

- six, the passage of time: given the standard of proof (beyond a reasonable doubt), it becomes increasingly difficult to convict years after a crime. Witnesses move, disappear and eventually die. Their evidence often deteriorates. They can be more successfully cross-examined. Forensic evidence (which may be enhanced by new techniques) is more likely to be lost or destroyed with years of storage;

- and seven, resources: the lord chief justice of NI (Sir Declan Morgan)[9], the local attorney general (John Larkin QC)[10] and the chief constable (George Hamilton)[11] have variously indicated that concentrating upon the past means, the criminal justice system cannot deal properly with the present. It follows that NI may have a bleak future, which has been distorted by a bad past and has not been better prepared in a post-troubles present.

There has been little spontaneous reconciliation since 1998, even though violence has given way to politics. It is very striking that, for many, time has not healed. This is not helped by the perception that 'bad guys' – including the OTRs – do well in NI. But the instinctive response, to investigate and prosecute all perpetrators (even with only two years in prison), is extremely problematic. We only have the PSNI's Operation Redfield at present, which

---

[9] *Belfast Telegraph,* 17 November 2014; BBC, 18 January 2016 (referring to the 56 pending inquests).

[10] Various media interviews & press reports, 19-20 November 2013.

[11] Speech to British-Irish association, 6 September 2014.

is looking again at all the OTR cases. And the number of successful prosecutions, after further abuse of process applications, and various defences, is not likely to satisfy many people.

Amnesty

The following are important arguments, for or against amnesty:

- one, precedent: the new Irish state legislated three times in 1923-24, to protect from civil and criminal liability: UK forces; republicans in the war of independence; and free state forces in the civil war. Early in the NI troubles, the Stormont government announced an executive amnesty, for the period 5 October 1968 to 6 May 1969[12];

- two, immunities: there has long been special treatment of republicans: between 1997 and 2010, regarding the decommissioning of terrorist weapons; between 1998 and 2013, regarding evidence to the Saville inquiry, and the four lesser ones (Robert Hamill, Rosemary Nelson, Billy Wright, and Breen and Buchanan); and from 1999 and continuing, regarding the recovery of the disappeared[13];

- three, the 1998 Belfast agreement: the NIO did not prepare in advance of the talks for the release of terrorist prisoners. Sinn Féin handled the issue badly, failing to look after a complex republican constituency.[14] It did

---

[12] Lord Trimble suggested there was early release of prisoners after the 1956-62 IRA campaign: NIAC, *Report*, Q807, 13 May 2014.

[13] President Clinton may have had a hand in this: see his telephone calls to Tony Blair, on 8 and 23 May 1998, following a meeting with WAVE representatives (Clinton presidential library and museum, collection no. 2012-0600-M).

[14] Its comprised the following prisoners: (i) those sentenced in NI before 1973; (ii) those sentenced in NI since 1973; (iii) transferees to NI;

not even demand an amnesty. The text of the agreement was inadequate, and caused problems subsequently. By not signing up to the Belfast agreement, the republicans had no hope of political support for prisoner releases (OTRs did not even register). They certainly gave nothing positive in return for what the UK, and Irish, government gave them in 1998-2000;

- four, statutory amnesty: it was Lord Williams of Mostyn, followed by Lord Goldsmith, who put the idea on the agenda after the Belfast agreement, albeit negatively in advice to Tony Blair;

- five, officialdom: the NIO, and in particular Sir Quentin Thomas, came up with the idea of excluding the security forces from an amnesty, this idea prevailing between 2001 and 2005;

- and six, legislation: the government's Northern Ireland (Offences) bill was opposed by all other parties in 2005-06, but Sinn Féin pulled the plug when it could no longer deny that the security forces were to be included.

The story of the OTRs reveals missed opportunities. The UK (and Irish) government failed to include an amnesty (really two) in the Belfast agreement. Sinn Féin, of course, wanted special treatment, without signing up to the Belfast agreement or having to decommission. The failure of public policy was the subsequent appeasing of the republicans in a less than transpar-

---

(iv) transferees to the Republic of Ireland; and (v) escaped prisoners from mainly NI. Sinn Féin went on to elide the following OTRs subsequently: (vi) those subject to extradition requests to the Republic of Ireland and other countries; (vii) volunteers who had not been arrested, and may or may not have been on the run; and (viii) political militants, not members of the IRA, who had helped criminally.

ent peace process. The idea of excluding the security forces had been Sir Quentin Thomas's; ironically, this is the card Sinn Féin played to destroy the Northern Ireland (Offences) bill.

Prosecution versus Amnesty

Any discussion of prosecution versus amnesty will have to take account of the factors listed above, and no doubt others. The prediction regarding prosecution is most likely: whatever of the efforts of the legacy litigators (who are keen on state killings), there will be no general refighting of the troubles through the courts in coming years. The prospects of any amnesty are, of course, slight, given a continuation of the present political standoff. It would be going further than the Belfast agreement. When it was tried in 2005-06, only the labour government and Sinn Féin supported it (until the republicans turned against).

We now know that Tony Blair's secret diplomacy led only to the Downey fiasco. The 228 OTRs are being reviewed, with a view to successful prosecution. This is the PSNI's operation Redfield. And it is associated with the replacement of the historical enquiries team by the so-called legacy investigation branch of the police service. Maybe circumstances will emerge, where the idea of properly drawing a line under the past, appeals to different groups, albeit for different reasons. Sinn Féin, out to get the security forces (not that there are likely to be many cases), would be opposed to the principle of equal treatment of all criminal suspects. But do the 228 OTRs want to continue running personal risks, on the slight chance that a member of the security forces – who acted unlawfully – will be prosecuted successfully?

The emergence of the statute of limitations lobby, with roots in the military community, could be significant. On one view, it is OTRs mark 2, with republican terrorists replaced by members of the security forces. On another view, the perceived risks for the 228 IRA members (now privately pensioned presumably), and the articulated fears of many more soldiers (most of whom acted perfectly lawfully), could constitute two different reasons, in the right political context, for my drawing of a line under the past – a responsible act of statecraft, inspired not by amnesia but by desire to tell more truth based upon the huge archives in London, Belfast and Dublin.

This advocacy of an amnesty is not designed to lock relatives and survivors into their private worlds of grief, while the rest of NI gets on with its life. Yes, inquests, investigations and prosecutions would stop. But, and this is crucial to the idea I am advocating, there would then be an opening of the archives, subject to human rights concerns. The outstanding precedent is the 2012 *Report of the Hillsborough Independent Panel*[15], into the 1989 Sheffield football tragedy which saw 96 Liverpool fans killed. Relatives and survivors would learn much more than might emerge in a criminal court. The perpetrators might have to confront their past deeds. And society generally could begin to see more clearly who killed whom in the NI troubles.

Dealing with the Past

The Eames/Bradley report of 2009 did not survive for long.[16] It was a case of suicide, not murder! If the recommendations – based upon a legacy commission - had been accepted then, it would have been implemented over five years. Thus, the origin of the idea of dealing with the past in a finite period.

The Haass/O'Sullivan talks in late 2013 had not even achieved agreement.[17] But they left a list of new adopted institutions, with

---

[15] HC 581, 12 September 2012, 389 pp plus http://hillsborough.independent.gov.uk

[16] *Report of the Consultative Group on the Past,* 23 January 2009.

[17] Proposed Agreement 31 December 2013, *An Agreement among the Parties of the Northern Ireland Executive on Parades, Select Commemo-*

an alphabet soup of initials. On 23 December 2014, after eleven weeks of talks brokered by the NIO, the Stormont House agreement emerged in Belfast.[18]

The 2014 Stormont House Agreement

The Stormont House agreement was between principally the DUP and Sinn Féin: the alliance party supported it; but the Ulster unionist party and SDLP had reservations. It had the – mainly financial – support of the UK government, which makes a difference.

This agreement, under 'the past', provided for: one, an oral history archive; two, a historical investigations unit; three, a UK/ Irish independent commission on information retrieval; and, four, an implementation and reconciliation group.[19] The past, and legacy litigation, has become a major topic.

Strangely, OTRs was nowhere mentioned in the Stormont House agreement, after the official Hallett report (July 2014) on the administrative scheme but before the NI affairs committee of the house of commons reported, in March 2015.

A Fresh Start Agreement

Implementation of the Stormont House agreement was interrupted by two related IRA murders.[20] The UK government was forced to admit that the IRA still existed, but that it was com-

---

rations, and Related Protests; Flags and Emblems; and Contending with the Past.

[18] There is in fact: a principal agreement of 14 pages; and a 5-page financial annex.

[19] Paras 21 to 55.

[20] Gerard 'Jock' Davison, 5 May 2015; Kevin McGuigan, 12 August 2015.

mitted to Sinn Féin's political objectives.[21] There followed ten weeks of talks in NI.

On 17 November 2015, the NIO published: *A Fresh Start: the Stormont agreement and implementation plan* (67 pp). This document, agreed again principally by the DUP and Sinn Féin, dealt with some issues, such as finance, reform of Stormont and ending paramilitarism. However, it failed to deal at all with the past[22]: 'Despite some significant progress', the NIO stated, 'a final agreement on the establishment of new bodies to deal with the past was not reached. The Government continues to support these provisions of the Stormont House Agreement and to provide better outcomes for victims and survivors. We will now reflect with the other participants on how we can move forward and achieve broad consensus for legislation.'[23]

Historical Investigations Unit

The historical investigations unit – if it ever goes ahead - requires legislation.[24] It is to run for five years. And it will come under the NI policing board. Essentially, it is to be a merger of the PSNI's historical enquiries team (now the legacy investigation branch) and the historical investigations directorate of the police ombudsman. But the former has full police powers, while the latter has

---

[21] Lord Carlisle QC, Rosalie Flanagan & Stephen Shaw QC, *Paramilitary Groups in Northern Ireland*, 19 October 2015 (7 pp); HC, *Hansard*, vol. 600, cols. 829-42, 20 October 2015.

[22] Pp. 34-5.

[23] Press release, 17 November 2015; *Irish News*, 17 November 2015 (article by Therese Villiers on historical investigations unit and national security).

[24] The queen's speech, on 27 May 2015, referred to Westminster legislation. In September 2015, the NIO published a paper, *Northern Ireland (Stormont House Agreement) Bill 2015* (33 pp).

more limited ombudsman powers. The historical enquiries team's work was addressed to victims. The police ombudsman's work concerns retired political officers. OTRs are fugitive suspects. It may be assumed that Operation Redfield is to go to the historical investigations unit. The unit is to have a relationship – as part of the policing family – with the public prosecution service of NI.

The Stormont House agreement (as noted) envisaged three other institutions[25], as well as the historical investigations unit.

Perhaps the UK and NI governments (if ever restored) could try and advance those ideas separately. In advance of her appointment as first minister in January 2016, Arlene Foster (herself a troubles victim) showed the importance of information being disclosed.[26] And, despite the exclusion of the past, the NIO has unilaterally published the international agreement – with more special treatment of republicans - on the independent commission on information retrieval.[27]

Political Stalemate

It is unclear whether the period begun in January 2017, with the resignation of Martin McGuinness, and the collapse of the assembly, was due to end in February 2018, with Gerry Adams handing the presidency of Sinn Féin to Mary Lou McDonald. Certainly, Arlene Foster, in refusing to sign up to whatever was on offer, with London and Dublin looking on, denied McDonald the credit for the restoration of devolution at the beginning of her leadership.

---

[25] An oral history archive; a UK/Irish independent commission on information retrieval; and an implementation and reconciliation group.

[26] *Belfast Telegraph,* 18 December 2015.

[27] HC, *Hansard,* vol. 604, cols. 43WS-44WS, 21 January 2016. This was signed on 15 October 2015. Article 9 is: inadmissibility of information received by the commission.

It is also unclear what the two leading parties might have agreed on the past, or not, though they are more likely to have added to, rather than, subtracted from the list of legacy bodies (with all those initials), and armies of bureaucrats and quango-crats ready to be deployed.

Conclusion

Back to Civil Society

It is my view that we should stop waiting for restoration, and the continuing process begun with the Belfast agreement. What better than to cherry pick the good bits from 1998, such as recon-ciliation, and start a long march on the road to a politically bro-kered, and legalized, amnesty. The troubles lasted thirty years. We are now twenty years beyond the Belfast agreement. Already, the generation entering adulthood in 1968, is passing. The changes are that: as more – especially paramilitary - old soldiers pass away; the more the living will see the sense in freeing the criminal jus-tice system of the present from the legacy of the past.

About the author

Austen Morgan is a barrister in London (at 33 Bedford Row) and Belfast. He is the author of a number of books, including

Labour and Partition: Belfast Working Class 1905-1923 (London 1987), *The Belfast Agreement: A Practical Legal Analysis* (Belfast 2000) and *Tony Blair and the IRA: the 'on the runs' scandal* (London 2016; available on Amazon and Kindle):

a.morgan@33bedfordrow.co.uk

A Victim's Perspective

Ken Funston

South East Fermanagh Foundation Advocacy Manager

There are have been a number of maps made over the years, showing in graphics how terrorism affected the various parts of Northern Ireland. Virtually all the border areas with the Republic of Ireland, the urban conurbations of Belfast and Londonderry, and east Tyrone, had the most deaths per head of population.

It is no coincidence that murders around the border were so high. Our near neighbour in the RoI was prepared to turn a 'blind eye' to the activities of the IRA who used the Republic as a safe haven, until the IRA also became a threat to the RoI in the mid to late 1980s.

It may seem that because there were 'only' 116 deaths in Fermanagh, those numbers appear relatively few, but the county is predominately a rural farming community. Out of the 116 deaths, the Provisional PIRA was responsible for 104, and Loyalists five. The police 'clear-up' rate in the county is approximately 5%, meaning 95% of murders are unsolved. Yet the PSNI have made it clear that they have no interest in investigating the past[1].

Coming from a family badly affected by Irish republican-inspired terrorism, and working as an advocate for the South East Fermanagh Foundation (SEFF), it was/is the use of violence by the IRA in Fermanagh that dominates the SEFF workload and the Advocacy Service for Innocent Victims (AfIV).

I therefore want to deal with the Provisional movement's strategy and how they continue to pursue their 'war' within society.

---

[1] Chief Constable George Hamilton, SEFF Conference 2016, Lough Erne Golf Resort.

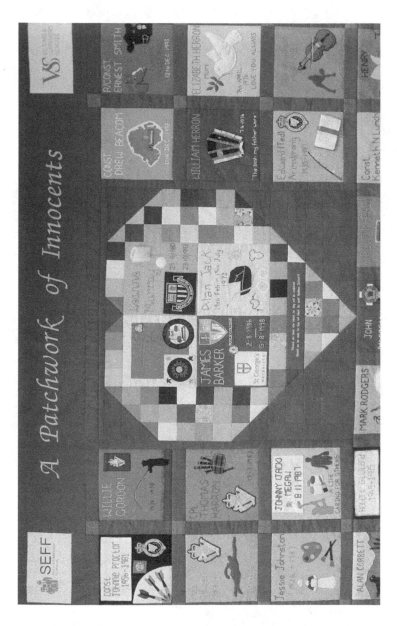

Section of 'A Patchwork of Innocents' memorial quilt (South East Fermanagh Foundation)

Section of 'Terrorism knows NO Borders' memorial quilt (South East Fermanagh Foundation)

Truth

Most political players demand truth from those they perceive as the other side, or sides, but seem unwilling to offer the truth from their side, or acknowledge and take responsibility for their actions. This is mostly because of fear that such acknowledgement will weaken them in the new dispensation and that the truth may be used against them within the context of the delicate peace that prevails[2].

The Provisional movement cannot and will not admit to their actions of the past. They have reached a moral standpoint where they have established an equivalence in that their members were quite simply responding to state terror. Gerry Adams will never admit to his involvement with the IRA, and the reality is a large section of the population now don't care or are ambivalent about his past.

I was recently present in the Dail giving a presentation to the Good Friday Agreement Implementation Committee[3] when quite a few senior members of Sinn Fein were present, including most of their MPs. Francie Molloy put forward the idea of a Truth Commission. The reality is they don't want any type of truth. It is easy for them to allege widespread collusion, but truth – I have no doubt the police and military hold many files implicating senior members of the Provisional movement in the most heinous of crimes – they can't handle the truth.

When I challenged Mr Molloy as to how a truth process would work, considering terrorist organisations do not hold documents

---

[2] Hamber B., 1998, Past Imperfect: Dealing with the Past in Northern Ireland and Societies in Transition, University of Ulster and IN-CORE.

[3] GFA Implementation Committee Meeting, 8 November 2017, Dail Eireann, Dublin.

or files, therefore they can minimise their involvement to as little as possible, he had no comeback.

Terminology

There is a sustained attempt by the Provisionals to introduce terminology into daily use that suits their narrative. This is served by academics that buy into this while the universities discourage calling a terrorist a 'terrorist'. Another example is how academics refer to an "ex-combatant" as an internationally recognised phrase which is generally used for both state and non-state actors who have been involved in violent conflict.

The definition equates the actions of the terrorist organisations with that of the state. However of the 3,500 deaths during the Troubles, republicans and loyalists are responsible for 90%; of the remaining 10% attributable to the state, a large proportion involved the legal taking of life as defined by Article 2 of the European Convention on Human Rights.

This is all part of the acceptable 'Troubles' language that has crept into society. I hear it in meetings with the Victims Commissioner and the Victims and Survivors Service when we are advised not to use the unacceptable 'terrorist' description but the other terms are never challenged.

In the Provo mind-set, and their loyalist cohorts, there was no other way. By their moral compass, I and thousands like me also had the right to take life in response to the murders of our own – the fact is, there was another way, and the vast majority of our society took the legal and moral route.

Definition of a Victim

That strategy moved on to the next level, and this is one that probably annoys victims more than any other – the definition of a victim. If the Provisionals can have their members accepted as equal combatants to those of the State, then they can be equal victims also.

'Reshape, Rebuild, Achieve'

The document *Reshape, Rebuild, Achieve* was produced in April 2002 by the Victims Unit of the Office of the First Minister and Deputy First Minister. Its co-signatories were Denis Haughey, SDLP, and James Leslie, UUP, on behalf of the then First Minister, David Trimble, and Deputy First Minister, Seamus Mallon. It identified victims as, "The surviving physically and psychologically injured of violent, conflict related incidents and those close relatives or partners who care for them, along with those close relatives or partners who mourn their dead"[4].

This was the seeming start of the communal victimhood, as perceived by Sir Kenneth Bloomfield[5] and Eames Bradley[6] that was to distress many of those we now term as 'innocent victims', i.e. those who through no fault of their own had become victims of terror.

The 2002 document metamorphosed into The Victims and Survivors (Northern Ireland) Order 2006.

Interpretation in the Order of a "victim and survivor"

3. (1) In this Order references to "victim and survivor" are references to an individual appearing to the Commissioner to be any of the following:—

---

[4] http://cain.ulst.ac.uk/issues/victims/docs/vu03.pdf

[5] http://cain.ulst.ac.uk/issues/violence/victims.htm

[6] http://cain.ulst.ac.uk/victims/docs/consultative_group/cgp_230109_report.pdf

a.   someone who is or has been physically or psychologically injured as a result of or in consequence of a <u>conflict-related incident</u>;

b.   someone who provides a substantial amount of care on a regular basis for an individual mentioned in paragraph (a); or

c.   someone who has been bereaved as a result of or in consequence of a <u>conflict-related incident</u>.

The next stage is for Republicans to gain pensions for their injured members. They do not mind if Loyalists also get these pensions. Once their 'test' cases pass through the system, the floodgates will open. Receiving such state pensions will legitimise their past. It is this abuse of the system by the terrorist organisations that is preventing many hundreds of innocents availing of a pension that they badly need, as they refuse to be morally equated with a terrorist.

Sinn Fein states it is committed to designating a Day of Reconciliation that "reflects different loyalties but which signals a commitment to building a better future"[7]. They recently held what was termed, 'A Time for Truth' black-flagged rally in Belfast that was quite concerning. I cannot speak for others but I hear the views of many innocent victims in the course of both my work and research. The people I engage with do not want to attend any type of rally, parade, or anything else that is clearly infiltrated by unapologetic terrorists of any persuasion who continue to deny their past. It was quite disappointing that victims of terror were used in this way.

---

[7]   https://www.sinnfein.ie/files/2016/ReconciliationDoc_2016.pdf

Consultation on the Stormont House Agreement Legacy Bill

When?
How?
Voiceless. Have the decisions been made, do our views matter?
Do the victims matter?
Issues with the Stormont House Agreement structures like the HIU; Statute of Limitations.

These are questions that must be answered before and during any Bill consultation process. Even though it is easy to be despondent, we must become involved in this process, and have our voices heard.

The American, Chuck Palahniuk stated, "You realise that our mistrust of the future makes it hard to give up the past."

Innocent Victims feel badly let down, both by our local politicians and British governments. We feel that 'we are in the way', that 'we need to move on', we are not considered in any legislation and policy, while giving victims' groups a level of funding might keep us quiet.

It was at the close of World War I, Edmund Wilson looked out over London and said, "No one pretends to give a damn anymore – unless they are one's close friends or relatives – whether people are killed or not ... The long-continued concentration on killing people whom we rarely confront, the suppression of the natural bonds between ourselves and these unseen human creatures, is paid by repercussions. The spitefulness and fear and stifled guilt, in our immediate personal relations ... Our whole world is poisoned now."[8]

---

[8] http://archive.vva.org/archive/TheVeteran/2005_03/feature_HistoryPTSD.htm

Dealing with our Future by Dealing with our Past: Properly or not at all?

Trevor Ringland LLB

The context

Northern Ireland is a truly beautiful place and its people recognised by those who visit as generally welcoming and friendly.

That such a people should become immersed in a deeply sectarian and racist conflict is a consequence of malign racial, religious, cultural and political leadership. No-one is born hating. It is taught!

In dealing with the consequences of the conflict, we must maintain a focus on the challenge to build a peaceful, stable and shared society in Northern Ireland, on this island and between these islands. Embedding a sense of interdependence among the people—a vital foundation upon which to build a successful society—should not just be an aspiration but an imperative. Success in this regard would surely be the greatest tribute we could pay to those who died or suffered loss and injury.

Let me begin by painting some context. First of all, we must be realistic and honest with the victims of violence, as to what can be achieved within the political reality of our 'peace process'.

In that light, a comment by Alan McBride, whose wife was killed in the Shankill Road bomb in 1993, is relevant: 'Without taking anything away from the personal responsibility of those who planted that bomb, I would also blame the sectarian society that created their mind-sets.'

Once the conflict broke out in the late 1960s, many young men and women acted in a manner contrary to their behaviour in a normal society. Harry's story emphasises this.

Harry's brother was shot by the army and it is difficult to understand in the circumstances why the soldiers responsible, when prosecuted, were not convicted. Harry, a teenager at the time, was understandably deeply embittered by the loss of his elder brother. Some republicans began to encourage him to seek revenge. Fortunately, his father recognised what was happening and packed him off to the United States, where he stayed for 18 months. During that time his understandable hurt eased. Otherwise Harry would accept he could have easily been drawn down the path taken by so many that led them into violence.

It is part of our tragic history that too many young people did not escape such influences, blighting their lives as well as those of their victims. This is not to excuse an individual's actions, including those of some members of the security forces, but it does help us understand why some acted in the way they did during the madness that we call the 'troubles'.

It would be my contention that for political expediency we have been doing everything possible to avoid dealing with the past and that is unsustainable and risks passing the baggage of our history on to future generations.

The fragmented manner in which it has been progressed to date is compounding the hurt and deepening fractures in our society.

The components of conflict

Now let us explore the sectarianism and cultural racism (variously anti-Irish and anti-British) which created the foundations for the conflict and, indeed, sustained it. This has the following main elements:—

Exclusive concepts of identity

To define Irishness or Britishness in exclusive ways ignores the reality of the existence of the two main traditions on this island, never mind the increasing diversity of its people, and so is hardly conducive to building an interdependent, peaceful and stable society. A variation on the words of the Ulster poet, John Hewitt, suggest a more inclusive approach and one that is properly reflective of the 'mongrel' nature of our make-up. Hewitt described himself thus:

A Belfast man

An Ulster man

An Irishman and British

And those last two are interchangeable

And I am European

And anyone who demeans any one part of me demeans me as a person.

These words help define our Northern Irishness and offer a fairly good template which can be adapted to reflect our increasingly ethnically diverse and hence the more socially complex identity of our society.

Imagination of the 'Other'

A major flaw in the construction of difference was the labelling of whole communities that you were opposed to as dangerous and damaging. In our society we too rarely challenged the stereotypes that we were given about the 'other' side. The idea that those on the 'other' side all felt the same way about conflict and wanted the same things was a nonsense but nonetheless a 'reality' in too many unchallenged minds. That imagination also included a middle class who saw the marginalised as the cause of conflict without realising they too played a defining role. A rebuilt society must challenge such myopia and create a space in which identities are more personal, as opposed to fixated upon mythic groups.

Religious intolerance

As Gandhi once said, 'When I read the scriptures I see Christ. When I meet Christians I don't!' If he had visited Ireland he might well have expressed such a view or as the Dalai Lama did say: 'Nowhere else in this world do two groups of Christians fight.' Ireland has provided examples of both the best and worst of religion. Killing your neighbour is certainly not at the core of the Christian message. Loving and treating your neighbour as you yourself would like to be treated are and show a better way of sharing the future—one where relationships are built rather than being destroyed.

Politics based on flawed ideologies

Politics, it is said, is about the pursuit of power. In addition it is too often about the manipulation of the masses by the relatively few, for their own benefit rather than that of the wider society, through populist and short-term policies.

In the future all sectors of our society should be more demanding, to ensure that those practising politics do so in a constructive way to secure the common good. In the past the politics of this island too often promoted fear, exclusion, division and victimhood through mutually exclusive nationalisms based on hatred of the other, rather than normal, left/right, issue-based policies. Those who simply wave a flag should be challenged on the paucity of their arguments and their inability to deal with the real issues that affect people's daily lives.

In the absence of the Civic Forum, the various interest groups that shape civic society—such as employers' organisations, the trade unions, the third sector, sporting bodies, churches, the media and education—need to play an active and constructive oppositional role, as 'critical friends' to elected representatives.

The constitutional issue can also be addressed by purely peaceful means, by building relationships rather than destroying them and through inclusion rather than exclusion. To argue for a Northern Ireland for all or a North of Ireland for all is the right thing to do, as well as strategically making sense depending on one's political perspective on the constitutional position of Northern Ireland. We should show little tolerance for any other method used.

In reality the only way to pursue a constitutional preference is through making this place we share work for the benefit of all its people.

Social structures

Leading separate lives is hardly conducive to a peaceful and stable society. Separate education, religion, culture and sport, and other aspects of a divided society, meant it was easy to demonise the other, as they were strangers. There was a failure to address issues such as discrimination, housing and gerrymandering. The Civil Rights Movement was, in its purest arguments, about making Northern Ireland a better place as opposed to the violent campaign of the IRA, which was about undermining and overthrowing the State as well as driving the 'British' into the sea.

Poverty and unemployment also create fertile ground for those promoting extremism. So too does a well-heeled group whose material position makes them immune to the realities of life for many. For the middle classes there is a poverty of both the mind and leadership. Hence building a strong economy and an inclusive society will play a vital role in building a shared and better future. A clear commitment needs to be given to that goal as an absolute imperative.

Violence

The history of Ireland and the relationships between these islands has too often, though by no means exclusively, been one of violence resulting in human tragedy and damaged relations. In a region with little more than 1½ million people the 'troubles' resulted in over 3,600 deaths, thousands more injured, an unmeasured numbers of suicides and stress induced deaths and over 20,000 imprisoned (over 12,000 republicans, over 8,000 loyalists). There was also a substantial dislocation of the population in areas of Belfast and Londonderry/Derry in particular and ethnic cleansing in some areas, leaving a legacy of a 'Balkanised' region. Its physical manifestations include some 100 'peace walls' and other communal barriers throughout Northern Ireland.

As we look to the future we have a choice. We can either work to break down the barriers, rebuild relationships and construct new ones or do nothing and somehow expect our society not to revisit violent conflict at some stage in the future. If we should have learned anything in Northern Ireland, however, it is that every death causes a ripple of hurt that passes down through the generations.

It is also worthwhile setting out the responsibility for the deaths, taken from the volume *Lost Lives*:

Republican paramilitaries	2,148
Loyalist paramilitaries	1,071
British Army	301
UDR	8
RUC	52

In turn, the following were killed:

Civilians	2,051
Army	503
UDR/RIR	206
RUC	312
Republican paramilitaries	394
Loyalist paramilitaries	157

Loyalist paramilitaries killed around 26 members of the IRA, while the IRA killed some 26 loyalists. Each organisation killed more of 'their own' than did anyone else.

Proposals

Dealing with the past must be supported by a strong commitment to reconciliation, to counter-balance the potential for those exposed by the process adopted to promote further conflict to cover their past actions. Yet our political classes too often take divisive positions, while reconciliation projects are driven from the ground up through various organisations and individuals, often at a very local level, lacking the political leadership required.

Politics at present is polarised but the people are not necessarily so. The challenge is how do we ensure the people de-polarise the politics before it polarises the people.

At the same time it is important that we recognise and hold to internationally recognised norms of democracy, human rights and the rule of law. In this respect I would suggest a 'Statement of Wrongs' should be drawn up. It was wrong where certain police officers and soldiers acted outside of the law and it was wrong of the IRA and the loyalist paramilitaries to use violence to further their aims. It was also wrong to promote exclusive identities of Irishness and Britishness and to feed the hatred of sectarianism and cultural racism. It was also wrong to silence those whose identity was more nuanced—those who could accept an Irish and a British dimension to their lives.

While some might argue that violence was necessary for the Republic of Ireland to gain its independence from the United Kingdom it was never the method through which to try and achieve a united Ireland. Or maintain N. Ireland as part of the United Kingdom.

Respected figures from civic society could be asked to draft this statement. The alternative is to continue the myth that the killings of Bloody Sunday, Kingsmills, Shankill, Greysteel or Warrenpoint and so many other such incidents, were right and justified.

While there should be a clear separation made between the pursuit of Truth and Justice and that of the creation of an opportunity for those whose lives, whether through loss of a loved one or serious injury, were impacted upon by the Troubles, a structure could be created to manage which path a particular case should take with the focus on bringing about resolution to each case as far as is possible.

The matter of Truth and Justice should have rested with the justice system. However, the two Governments, in looking to create convoluted structures, seem to be pursuing a course of determining how best to resolve justice issues by first and foremost being concerned as to how the application of the normal legal process might impact on the peace/political process.

So to begin with and before any further finance is spent and working within the existing structures, those impacted upon by the Troubles should have their story or personal truth listened to. Those involved could be divided into three groups

a) Civil Society

b) Members of the Security Forces

c) The Paramilitaries

It would be an opportunity for them to have their voice heard if they so wish and it would also hopefully humanise the suffering of so many.

It would from the outset create an effective form of story-telling inside a legal structure and could be easily established at reasonable cost. Bearing in mind it would be their version of the truth, our society would hear at first hand the experiences of those families so tragically affected by the madness of our conflict.

That initial hearing would then assist in determining how best to bring about a resolution to each case—bearing in mind the State's responsibilities under the European Convention on Human Rights and, in particular, article 2 guaranteeing the right to life.

It could be structured thus:

1. Additional Judges could be appointed to facilitate the hearings (Possibly supported by two suitably qualified lay appointees where appropriate).

2. Lawyers would be appointed to assist in the preparation and presentation of the evidence.

3. Witness evidence would be covered by privilege (through legislation if necessary), to enable as full disclosure as possible. While some names could be included in statements to be put before the judges, there could be restrictions on the use of names in the initial open forum unless those persons had already been convicted. Contempt proceedings could be brought against anyone who breached the rules.

4. The Chief Constable or his appointee could at the outset lay out the paramilitary structures, including the names of those in the positions of leadership, in each area from 1969 to date based on the intelligence infor-

mation available. Such information would also open up the option for a Nuremberg format trial of the leaderships of the various paramilitary organisations.

5. The number of witnesses would be restricted to those seriously injured or one member of the family of those killed (father, mother, sister, brother, son, daughter, spouse).

6. The Police and PPS would present the evidence in each case

7. The judge or Panel would also make recommendations arising out of the initial hearing as to how best the ECHR obligations could be met.

8. Each family would provide a short 'statement of impact' setting out the consequences that their loss or injury had on them and provide more information on those who died. The Thomas Niedermayer story is just one example. Murdered by the IRA in 1973, his wife, two daughters and one of their husbands all took their own lives. The actual deaths from our 'conflict' are considerably greater than currently recognised.

At that initial hearing the Judge or Panel would make recommendations as to how the investigation and justice process should continue in respect of each case.

Its determination on the evidence before it could:

a. Conclude that nothing further could or should be done in a case.

b. Hold that the case could still be pursued to the criminal standard of proof of 'beyond reasonable doubt'.

c. Hold that while it was highly unlikely the criminal standard of proof would be met a finding of fault could be made on the civil standard of 'balance of probabilities' as in the Omagh case and where appropriate, an award of damages made against those responsible.

d. A 'determination of truth' could be made subject to genuine National Security concerns and if necessary through a hearing similar to an Inquest.

e. Cases involving those whose deaths that were caused by members of the security forces could have them dealt with in a way to ensure that the families are provided with independent investigation and decision around prosecution but any cases would still be heard in our justice system.

f. Mediation could be used where appropriate to help explain or resolve particular issues in cases

Where it is possible apologies should be issued by the State, through an agreed structure including the Retired Police Officers' Association and an army equivalent, for any deaths in which they have been involved and the person killed was entirely innocent. Such acknowledgment is important to remove any resulting stigma.

Loyalist and republican paramilitaries, as well as the security services when they acted outside the rule of law, should be encouraged to unambiguously apologise. To say 'sorry but it was justified' is unacceptable if we are genuinely striving to ensure that our children are not to repeat the mistakes of our past. A fulsome apology would contribute to reconciliation to some degree.

For consideration and bearing in mind that it is neither legal nor appropriate to give an amnesty to those who acted outside the rule of law, those who give such an apology could have their sentence suspended or reduced and the perpetrator released on licence.

For those who do not, then on conviction the sentence would be the normal for the crime they committed. Such an apology would have to be given before any trial to benefit from the sentence reduction.

A Day of Private Reflection has already been held, being the 21st June, and it should be continued and its profile increased. The day could include a 'Promise' or 'Statement of Commitment'—to be made by individuals, in schools, in churches and so on—to our society and in particular the victims of the 'troubles', that we will work to ensure that we never again allow violence to be used as a means of determining relationships between the people of this island.

The practical needs of victims and survivors in respect of their health and social requirements should be dealt with by the Victims Commissioner, though such provision should be based around need. This includes a pension for the injured and provision made for mental health.

In 'dealing with the past' so far we have stumbled through in an unsatisfactory and disjointed way, with an imbalance to the investigations, inquiries and inquests that have been or are to be carried out. This is unsustainable and if not managed fairly could destabilise the progress that has been made by our society to date.

The reason why I believe we have to deal with the past is that the considerable grace that has been shown by so many to allow our 'peace Process' to evolve has been at best underappreciated but in reality treated with disdain and hence wasted. How many are aware that over 700 murders of security force members remain unsolved!

So while politically we have been attempting to avoid dealing with the past we have also failed to promote reconciliation with the sense of purpose necessary to move a society deeply impacted by conflict to a more stable and genuinely shared future.

Political leadership has been lacking at governmental level as well as locally. To have addressed the following might have opened up the opportunity to deal with the past differently.

A. As outlined above call the use of violence outside the law to pursue a constitutional preference as wrong and unjustified.

B. Clear commitment to make NI work as the only means by which to pursue a constitutional preference.

C. Genuinely shared and integrated education and housing rolled out across NI.

D. A pension for the 390 innocent injured victims (separate provision considered for the 10 injured paramilitaries).

E. Paramilitary murals removed and their organisations disbanded. Any commemorations of members carried out sensitively and in private.

F. Substantially increased sentences for terrorist related offences post 1998 particularly for murder of police officers.

G. UK-Irish extradition streamlined.

H. The restructuring of the Assembly to allow for three groupings and any two of three can govern. All three entitled to be in the Executive but opposition option available.

I. Re-establishment of the Civic Forum.

J. Strategic investment and support for reconciliation projects.

K. Strict management of suspected terrorists in society.

L. A clear definition of collusion adopted. It has to be a crime.

M. Full support for the Proposals of the Working Group on Paramilitarism.

N. A Peace Centre that sets out the facts and consequences of conflict.

O. An apology from the two Governments and local party leaders for the mistakes of the past that fed the hatred at the heart of our conflict including a clear statement that violence was never the way to promote good relationships across these islands and should certainly never be used or tolerated again.

This is not an exhaustive list.

The alternative is not to do any of the above in respect of pursuit of justice. While an amnesty is not legally possible, there could be a general suspension into all investigations into the past for say fifty years, whether criminal, civil, through Inquests or Police Ombudsman. This would leave the only option being a limited 'truth' forum to take evidence of the impact of each death on the families.

There is little basis currently for such a proposal being recommended.

Concluding comments

One cannot equate the bomber with the bombed. Having said that, because of the mess that our society got into, it is important that all of those who suffered, no matter who they are, should be looked after. That would be part of ensuring that we take this opportunity, so that never again does this island turn to violence to resolve its political or social differences.

The internationally accepted definition as outlined in the European Framework Decision (2001/2002/JHA) on the standing of victims, adopted on 15th March 2001 and which defined a victim as,

> ‹a natural person who has suffered harm, including physical or mental injury, emotional suffering or economic loss, directly caused by acts or omissions that are in violation of the criminal law of a Member State.'

should now be adopted.

At times one wonders whether we have asked too much of ourselves in what we have had to accept, rightly or wrongly, to move our society away from conflict. The words of Michael Longley in his poem 'Ceasefire' perhaps best capture this, when King Priam asks for his son Hector's body to be released to him:

> I get down on my knees and do what must be done
> And kiss Achilles' hand, the killer of my son.

Our child is Northern Ireland and so many victims have quietly allowed our Peace Process to unfold and for that they should be thanked. Through the suggestions in this paper I hope they might help to ensure that important norms are established which create a foundation for a genuinely shared future for all of us.

We might also reflect on the words of Krystyna Chiger, a Polish Jew who survived the Holocaust. Asked in a recent interview whether she bore any resentment to the Germans, she replied: 'I don't feel any anger towards the younger generation. They should not suffer because of what their grandparents and parents did.'

Many of us have much to be angry about. But the challenge is surely to ensure that we do not let that anger shape the views of our children, to the extent that it blights their future as well as ours.

We have wasted grace but the future can be different and be one where we value each other's children as if they are our own.

We should set out now to deal with the future as suggested above and do so with maturity.

About the author

Trevor Ringland MBE is a Partner in the firm of Macaulay & Ritchie, Solicitors, in Belfast having studied law at Queen's University Belfast. Born in Belfast in 1959 he is married to Colleen with three children. He played rugby for Queen's University Belfast, Ballymena, Ulster, Ireland and the British and Irish Lions. He is currently Chairman of PeacePlayers-NI which uses sport and primarily basketball to promote good relations in Northern Ireland. He is a member of the British Irish Association and a founder member of the pro Union Group *Re-Union* which promoted a positive vision of Unionism and was a former member of the East Belfast Ulster Unionist Association and Co-Chairman of the *One Small Step* campaign, promoting a shared future for the people of Northern Ireland. He is a Director of the Ireland Funds, Co-operation Ireland, BCSDN and Peace Players International (NI) (Chairman). He served on the Sports Council, Broadcasting Council for Northern Ireland and the Irish Rugby Football Union. He was also a Trustee of the RUC George Cross Foundation and a former non-executive Director of Independent News & Media (NI) Ltd. He co-authored a pamphlet *The Long Peace. A future vision for Unionism* with Mick Fealty and David Steven and was a member of the Policing Board for Northern Ireland. He is a member of Knock Presbyterian Church.

Trevor was awarded the MBE in recognition of his cross-community work.

Mishandling of Legacy - One of the Biggest Scandals in the UK since the 2nd World War

Ben Lowry, Deputy Editor *The News Letter*

This week (ending March 3 2018) was a pretty standard week when it comes to legacy developments in Northern Ireland.

Two judges decided that prosecutors had been wrong not to charge a soldier over a Troubles shooting in Londonderry.

Last year the reverse happened in a case: a judge threw out an attempted murder charge against a soldier over a historic shooting but the Director of Public Prosecutions reinstated it.

Also this week, the BBC had yet another news investigation into circumstances around an alleged case of 'collusion' – in this case a surgeon who is backing someone who says he was forced out of the Army because he raised concerns about collusion.

Week after week after week, we read of some setback for the state in legacy matters for the Troubles.

Occasionally we hear of some success for the state but it usually just means that a republican legal action has failed, or perhaps been overturned at appeal.

In other words, success for the state merely means the republican narrative advance, so lavishly and endlessly funded by the state, has advanced at a slower pace.

The scandal of a state helping such a poisonous narrative when it actually prevented civil war and a determined and ruthless IRA campaign to terrorise an ethnic group in Northern Ireland and to subvert democracy in the United Kingdom, up to and including trying to blow the cabinet to smithereens, first

Ulster Unionists are right to be alarmed at latest on legacy

NC   27/2/18

Republicans were marching in Belfast yesterday. The event appeared on the main late evening national BBC news last night, and was described in a way that made it sound as if it was a general event attended by a representative cross section of victims. If it had been, most of the people present would have been victims of republican terrorism.

The report then referred to legacy inquests, as if Troubles victims were suffering some mysterious delay, without any hint that most such inquests will be into victims of the state.

The BBC Northern Ireland report was entirely different and much more comprehensive while the national report was brief. But if the BBC national news thinks such an event important enough to be broadcast in a UK-wide bulletin, it needs to give a greater sense of its flavour, in which republican black flags were flying and people were carrying banners that had messages such as 'Murdered by UFF/MI5'.

Sinn Fein is stepping up the rhetoric on the legacy of the Troubles. It had such success whipping up ill feeling over the Irish language that it has been little noticed that they were on the verge of getting funds for legacy inquests (quite aside from their alleged deal with London which would have ditched a statute of limitation for soldiers in legacy consultations).

This is all happening without any financial sum for how much inquests will soak up from the overall legacy funds.

It is reassuring to hear some voices speaking out against this madness. The former Ulster Unionst leader Lord Empey has picked up on a subtlety in the government's language on the consultation. It is talking about how the structures will be implemented, not on whether they are worthwhile.

If this process ends in moral equivalence between IRA and state, as there is reason to fear it will, it will be a searing betrayal of terror victims, the security forces and the UK itself.

The Ulster Unionist Party is entirely right to oppose such a process.

Belfast News Letter, Morning View, February 27 2018

There is still no clarity on the cost of legacy inquests

NL   9|3|18

The ruling in the High Court in Belfast yesterday on the bid for an inquest into the Loughgall killings in 1987 is one of the most significant developments to date on the legacy of the Troubles.

Sir Paul Girvan's judgement ran to many pages, and it will take some time to digest its implications.

In summary, he found that Arlene Foster, the DUP leader and then first minister, was wrong to take into account the absence of an overall agreed package to deal with legacy when she rejected funding for the inquests.

A likely consequence of the finding is a scenario that this column highlighted yesterday: that the legacy inquests will proceed without a clear understanding of how many inquests there will ultimately be and how much they will cost.

The inquests have to happen, we have been told by a host of different voices and experts, because governments must hold investigations into deaths at the hands of state forces that are compliant with Article Two of the European Convention on Human Rights.

This is so, but there are also lawyers who say that the obligation under Article Two can be met via investigations that fall short of separate inquests. The said inquests might cost as much as £1 million per hearing.

This then raises a serious question of proportionality, given that there are 1,000+ unsolved killings from the Troubles, most of which were at the hands of terrorists.

The government might well be so spooked by yesterday's hearing that it simply releases the money. It seems that the DUP and Conservatives were already inclined to do that.

If, however, this leads to a situation in which dozens of terrorists killed by the state (an investigation by this newspaper found that around 40 of the 90+ inquest dead were terrorists) ultimately get a greater level of funding and scrutiny than the funding and scrutiny allocated to those that they and their terror groups murdered, it will be a grave injustice for which those who approve funding will one day have to account.

Belfast News Letter, Morning View, 9 March 2018

in Brighton in 1984 and then in Whitehall itself in 1991, that scandal rolls on and on and on with minimal comment.

Take those two developments this week and then try to imagine parallel developments having happened.

Imagine that this week it had emerged that a senior republican and Sinn Fein figure will indeed face prosecution for terrorist charges of the utmost gravity.

Or try to imagine that this week the BBC had decided that the whole sweeping application of the word collusion was so potentially misleading, and such a powerful aide to the IRA narrative of the Troubles of British brutality, that it needed an entire documentary of its own.

I am not suggesting that the BBC should take any one view of the Troubles, such as the view that I might have or any one person in this room or elsewhere. I am just suggesting that having done so much reporting on collusion claims or findings that it might produce an entire documentary, just one, to consider the matter from another angle.

From this angle: Could it be the case – just *could* it be the case – that the word is being used to imply calculated, active state support for loyalist murder when in actual fact proven instances of collusion often relate to failures in the prevention or detection of such terrorism?

Such a single documentary from that perspective could easily be justified given there is a large number of influential people who believe that that is exactly how the word collusion is being misused.

It would go some way to balance the many news reports and BBC investigations that have taken collusion at face value, and take the assumed fact of collusion as their starting point.

The BBC have been good to me, in the sense that they try to give a platform to the viewpoint that I am trying to articulate and they often have me on a wide range of shows. But they seem never even to consider that they might be looking through the whole question of collusion from the wrong prism.

For be very clear about one thing. The single greatest aide to the pro IRA narrative is the collusion lie.

The lie that the British state in cahoots with loyalists engaged in wholesale murder and mayhem.

The lie is easily disproved (yet so rarely disproved by commentators who would merely need to summarise the numbers of dead in the Troubles by victim category).

I used merely to call it a myth. Eighteen months ago I wrote a piece entitled 'The Growing Myth of Loyalist Collusion' after the highly misleading way that the second Loughinisland's report finding of collusion – commissioned after the first report failed to find the said collusion – was relayed in the media.

The very clear impression that has been sent out was that the RUC facilitated and supported that 1994 loyalist massacre, despite the fact that near the top of the report it confirms that there was no evidence that police knew the attack was about to take place.

Then, recently, as the supposed fact of collusion at Loughinisland was again highlighted and emphasised, this time in the film No Stone Unturned, someone in the Twittersphere mockingly retweeted my article, 'The Myth Of Loyalist Collusion'.

His belief was that the documentary was yet another piece of evidence of collusion that showed that my view was so absurd that the retweeting my piece about, 'The Myth of Loyalist Collusion' would embarrass me.

Well, not only does it not embarrass me, and not only do I not resile from that article, I have moved on to refer to the collusion 'lie' rather than the myth.

It is such a distortion of events and it is so damaging to the state's record that it must be called out very clearly as the lie that it is.

Since I first started writing about this years ago I have always made clear my unequivocal view that there were instances of collusion.

There were instances indeed of the very worst collusion, in which the state illegally murdered people or elements of the state set people up for murder.

I remember well the period beginning around 1989, around the time of the vile murder of Pat Finucane, when as a student I was watching events closely and when loyalist intelligence suddenly seemed to get good.

Shootings such as that of Eddie Fullerton in Donegal, using a boat across the Foyle, or at Cappagh in 1991 when the UVF shot dead three IRA men.

But even from the earlier decades of the Troubles we know about the Glenanne Gang and the Miami Showband. We know that there were loyalists in the security forces.

No person with any credibility would deny that there were many instances of illegality and collusion.

My point is that they were many in absolute terms, scores of cases, but tiny in proportionate terms, out of the 3,700 overall killings.

The abiding fact about loyalist terrorism is how bad its intelligence was. By some accounts less than 50 of the 1,100 people murdered by loyalists were republican paramilitaries.

Given that 97% of the UDR was Protestant, many of whom had a clearly loyalist culture, and given that 90% of the RUC, which particularly in its reserve had a unionist culture, and given that these soldiers and police officers often had calling cards that identified suspects that they should be looking out for, it is surprising that loyalists were not routinely tipped off as to the details of republicans, resulting in the latter being killed illegally.

The facts of what happened in the case of the UDR Four of course has long been disputed but if we take the alleged case in outline then it is notable that such cases didn't happen several times a night, hundreds of times a year, thousands of times in the Troubles – in which security force members with information on republicans took the law into their own hands.

This is particularly so given that the community at large, let alone the people on the ground, saw the extent to which some of the most determined and skilled IRA terrorists outwitted the authorities and ran rings round the criminal justice system's need to prove guilt beyond all reasonable doubt.

The community at large was very annoyed about it, let alone the security force members who saw it up close, who knew the people who were getting away with murder, and who knew that the murderers would particularly target them, as security force members.

We know from societies all round the world, through history, that vigilantism is at risk of appearing if there is a perception that the authorities will not secure justice against the worst wrong-doers.

The big story about the British state and the Troubles is how restrained it was, despite many lapses, the most notable and shameful of which was on Bloody Sunday in 1972.

Again, when I express this obvious truth it is immediately distorted, and is daily being thrown back in my face.

Republicans will cite, or indeed get a grieving relative of a victim of the British army to cite, my comment about this security force restraint, as if an instance in which a thuggish soldier was trigger happy – and there were clearly some such instances – disproves my overall point about the record of the 300,000+ people who passed through Northern Ireland on duty during Operation Banner.

Has there ever been a situation like it in human history?

Has there been one, in which 2,100 killings by an insurgent group were met with a much lower number of killings in response by a much more powerful force?

A very small number of killings by the official force, many of them in public order situations in the chaotic early 1970s. Then a much larger number by loyalist groups, the striking feature of which is their attempt to strike at the community from which they believed the republican violence stemmed, rather than the more difficult task of striking at the leaders and perpetrators of that violence.

Has there previously been a situation in which the determination of an insurgent group to bomb and shoot its way to the destruction of the lawful authority has been met with an almost equal determination of that lawful authority, over many years, to adhere to the rule of law?

A determination such that the state accepted that a certain number of known and fanatical mass murderers would enjoy freedom of movement and freedom of association despite their flagrant guilt, because the state accepted that that guilt could not be proven in court, and that it would not accept alternative methods such as internment (after 1975) or by illegally killing them.

And again, when I make this point, republicans immediately distort it. They say that I am praising the state for not killing people illegally, for doing what the state forces are supposed to do and adhering to the rule of law.

No, no, that is not what I am doing.

It is they, by making the claim of brutality, who bring the issue up. It is we who are then obliged – obliged – to defend the state against these claims, rather than praise it. Defend it because of the distortions and the gross exaggerations of the state's record.

Both the two scenarios that I envisaged at the top of this address, which might bring some small balance to the direction of travel on legacy – the arrest and charge of an IRA leader or a sceptical BBC examination of collusion – could happen in the morning, we are sometimes pleasantly surprised by events, but none of us have come to think such developments are likely.

There is now an almost settled narrative of the Troubles: IRA violence versus collusion, the latter being a British state and loyalists who operated in concert – a joint enterprise that is no less than you would expect in a statelet that was sectarian to its very foundations.

That this narrative has been given so much weight by the British state itself, both in terms of funding but also in the way that it has been only lightly challenged by London – a reticence that is rooted in British decency and politeness in the face of embittered propagandists who are backed in their distortions by fools – is one of the biggest scandals since World War Two.

I have not a moment's hesitation in saying this.

The way in which the British state has turned in on itself over the story of the Troubles is seemingly a display of ostentatious fair play – 'look, look, how fair we are!' – taken to a level that tips into madness.

It is an immense scandal.

I say the biggest since the Second World War because The Troubles itself was, obviously, one of the largest and longest running challenges that the UK faced since 1945.

On the whole it is clear that after a confused and improvised response to an emergency, the state largely, particularly after 1973 or 1974, acquitted itself and saw off the determined republican violence without overly antagonising the nationalist community or the population in the Republic of Ireland.

It knew, after the disasters of Bloody Sunday and the botched first internment, that if it was ruthless in its response to the IRA it would radicalise the entire nationalist community, and also the Republic, and that we would have entered a disastrous period of perpetual war.

The violence fizzled out over time until its perpetrators no longer had the stomach for it and were instead brought into the democratic system.

No sensible person would every attribute the blame for the origins or the entirety of the Troubles to any one side of the tribal divide or any one group or faction. Of course the blame and blunders were spread all around.

And yet the course of the Troubles quickly became apparent.

There is a very important civil action that has been instigated against the killers of the three Scottish soldiers in the honey trap murders of March 1971, and which the News Letter is backing.

Those calculated murders, which caused revulsion across Britain and Ireland, were one of the most significant turning points, one of the key moments in the breach between soldiers and the nationalist community that they had arrived in part to protect.

There had only been 58 Troubles deaths prior to the honey trap murders. Republicans cannot blame or justify those three murders on British oppression such as internment, which did not happen until that summer, or on Bloody Sunday, which did not happen until the following January.

While much of the Troubles was chaos, this was one of the many republican moments of deep calculation, of the instilling of pure terror. It was possible in large part because soldiers were still at that time relaxed about their security.

So what do we see with the IRA?

Alongside this calculated targeting of soldiers, a bombing strategy to cause terror, centred initially on Belfast.

Consider the magnificent St George's Church on High Street, one of the finest buildings on this island, damaged nine times in 1972 alone. This cultural damage of course is of no consequence in comparison to the human agony caused by grievous crimes such as the Abercorn and Bloody Sunday bombings. And remember not just the deaths, but the horrific maimings, the many loses of limbs and eyes at the Abercorn alone, the appalling depravity of that attack as people chatted and had coffee on a Saturday, leading to 130 injured victims.

There were many such bombings. I was talking with colleagues last year and got confused between IRA bombs at the two newspapers where I have spent almost 20 years working, the Belfast Telegraph and the News Letter, so I checked what happened where: in the News Letter attack seven people were slaughtered in 1972 (none staff, but the dead included people who were trying to get away from the scene, such as a man, 65), at the 1976 Belfast Telegraph bombing only one died (an employee).

Through the 1970s the IRA killed members of the security forces, while continuing to bomb. Note how when they made 'mistakes' at La Mon for example or Enniskillen in the 1980s it was Protestant civilians who died.

In the 1980s, to step up the sense of terror, politicians were murdered, including Edgar Graham and Robert Bradford MP, as the INLA had murdered Airey Neave, to terrorise the prime minister, then trying to blow up the government at Brighton.

With regard to the heinous murder of Edgar Graham, which achieved so much of its goal of spooking a generation of unionists away from politics, it is very good to see Anne Graham here today.

The bombings on the mainland in the 1980s were calculated: from Hyde Park to Harrods to Deal to Brighton.

In the 1990s they became all the more so: huge economic bombs, on the calculation that vast sums of money might change minds and policies after all the bloodshed had not done.

In Northern Ireland too: the heart blown out of prosperous, mainly unionist towns such as Bangor and Coleraine.

Meanwhile, in Northern Ireland the fact that the security forces had become so good at protecting themselves pushed the terror in another direction. Those who were working with or supplying the armed forces were to be murdered: Patsy Gillespie, Teebane.

Don't forget the targetting of civil servants, including blowing up Sir Ken Bloomfield in his Crawfordsburn home using a number of devices that damaged neighbouring properties.

And what happened through the 1980s and 1990s?

This mixture of British and Ulster stoicism and restraint meant that the people who lived through the IRA, and the people on behalf of whom it was purported to be fought, nationalists in Northern Ireland, and the society the IRA wanted us by violence to join, the Republic, repudiated Sinn Fein, the political wing of the IRA. Solidly so in the nationalist community, around two thirds of Catholics voting for other parties. Overwhelmingly so in the Republic, where the Sinn Fein vote was between 1% and 4%.

The British response of discipline and moderation and normalisation saw off the calculated bombers and sectarian psychopaths, who finally sued for peace.

And now, in a response that is a mixture of moral collapse and near insanity, it is handing the IRA the narrative.

As one man in a position of authority put it to me, even some senior people in the security forces are guiding republicans by the hand to where they want to go on legacy.

I could go on and on about this but will finish on two points:

One, the final proof of failure, of abject surrender on legacy, is the fact that republicans are so confident that the coming legacy structures, agreed at Stormont House in 2014, will be good for them that they not only made legacy inquests a non-negotiable demand for the return of Stormont, but the DUP and London were clearly about to agree that demand.

Neil Faris's analysis, for example, that the Article 2 obligation under the European Convention on Human of Rights can be met without separate inquests, cast aside.

It was a News Letter analysis that found that around 40 of the 92 mooted legacy inquests will be into the deaths of terrorists. The inquests are expected to cost perhaps £1 million each.

This, among other injustices, will lead to the unpardonable situation in which the killings of the Loughgall IRA murder gang stopped by the SAS in 1987 will get a greater level of scrutiny than most of their 50+ victims, isolated border Protestants slaughtered by serial killers well known to the state but too accomplished in their murderous abilities to be convicted to the criminal standard.

And consider this chilling fact about the Historical Investigations Unit, HIU, the only body that might bring some balance to the legacy process and might turn the spotlight on the terrorists who did almost all of the illegal killing:

we are in the extraordinary situation that London has been scrambling to ensure that the HIU will in fact investigate things in a proportionate manner, and not itself turn in on the state forces, just as republicans want, because the state is easier to pursue because it has records.

Two, to people who would say what would you do differently, then I would say, if we do not take the approach suggested by Austen Morgan, of leaving legacy to the historians, then it must be made crystal clear to the IRA that if they are going to rake over the past it will be an uncomfortable process for them.

For example, London could quite simply have ordered a public inquiry into the IRA: time limited, costing say £100 million, i.e. half the price of the Bloody Sunday inquiry and a tiny fraction of it in per death costs. It would be much less unwieldy that the current historic sex abuse inquiry, it would be taking advantage of all the security force and state experts who are still alive to get to the bottom of who it was who ran this organisation and who it was who carried out its worst atrocities and how much damage Dublin's shameful extradition failures cause, and how we can learn from the overall experience of the long IRA onslaught to improve our response to a similar conspiracy in future.

Or, more simply, it could fund multiple civil cases, as belatedly it has done in the Hyde Park bombings, as it has not done in Birmingham, as it has not done in the soldier honey trap trio case, but as it is doing in so many republican legal cases in Northern Ireland.

APPENDICES

The Post-Truth Past and the Inverted Present

Arthur Aughey

There is genuine frustration in what might be called 'Middle Ulster' – a term of art which includes not only Unionists but also those Nationalists not seduced by Sinn Fein mantras – about the present condition of moral inversion: where terrorists have become victims; where those who enforced the law are now held to be criminals; where those who refused to support violence are held to be in debt to those who did; and where dealing with the past has come to mean underwriting a narrative of subversion. How do we explain how this situation developed?

It is tempting to think of this as being peculiar to our own time and distinctive of the warped present here. Of course, Northern Ireland's case has its own appalling character but the syndrome has a universal character and it has a history.

Appalled by not only the excesses of the French revolutionaries but also by the complicity of German academics and poets in romanticising and/or ignoring their effect, Hegel described the condition as 'a kind of slovenly sociability between sentimentality and badness'.

Slovenly sentimentality involves what we today would call virtue-signalling from a broad spectrum who emphasise peace, goodwill and harmony. Those who take this position are often well-meaning and decent but the defining characteristic is the wish to be *un*troubled about the present (and this includes many in UK Government). A loaded term would be that they share a disposition to appease.

Badness comprises SF/IRA (and Loyalist paramilitaries by default) and involves a deeply-layered strategy to continue the 'war' by other means. The claims of the 'bad' are contradictory but so far they have been able to pursue that agenda with reasonable success. That is because the sea in which they swim is no longer that of terrorist sympathy alone. They have also now the sea of slovenly sentimentality.

There is a contradiction in this slovenly sociability between sentimentality and badness and yet it consolidates, rather than undermining, the agenda. It is this.

On the one hand, adjusting political culture in the interests of peace (the appeal to the virtuous wish to end the Troubles) has become the insistence that notions of right and justice should not apply. This substitution involves setting aside the rule of law and subordinating it entirely to the demands of politics (something which came out at the Downey trial).

Individuals responsible for violence can displace personal accountability, representing murder as part of the generalised 'human tragedy' of the Troubles (for which everyone was responsible). It was not choice or agency but conditions which made violence inevitable/necessary and you can't attribute responsibility to terrorists alone since there are no clean hands in Northern Ireland's history. Rights activists, community workers, journalists and academics nod their heads in agreement with that logic – such that the slovenly sociability between sentimentality and badness enables terrorists and their political advocates to dance away from the past.

On the other hand, if everyone was indeed caught up in a situation which explains everything, only some - ex-prisoners - have been held to account for their actions. It is now time for others to pay their dues. Those others are 'state actors' so far exempt. At the end of this vista may not be the gallows (as Edmund Burke also reflected on the consequence sentimentality and badness in the French Revolution) but it certainly means more inquests; more police ombudsman reports; more criminal case review referrals; and more Article 2 cases at the European Court of Human Rights. The object is to redeem history by setting the balance to rights – in this case to exonerate terror, to marginalise its effect and to condemn the police and army.

This split-mind syndrome is a relationship between a disposition to 'overcome the past' (let's move on) and the need to 'come to terms with the past' (let's go back). In short, Republicans and Loyalists want at one and the same time for people to move on (but only onto their ground) and to go back (in order to attribute blame and punish others).

Generally, the term for this is 're-writing history'. But there is another crucial aspect. It is that the institutions of law and administration – upon which any decent society depends for its measure of right – appear to be working against what most people think of as being just. This takes a number of forms.

First is the inversion of accountability. Recently, the onus for rehabilitation has become focused on others acquiescing in perpetrators' storytelling rather than perpetrators reflecting on how they could have chosen alternative ways of acting. It also involves a slovenly sentimental adjustment to language – 'ex-combatants'; 'no hierarchy of victims' (except when it suits us); and so on.

Second is the related inversion of memory. Almost 15 years ago Labour MP John McDonnell argued that 'without the armed struggle of the IRA over the past 30 years' the Belfast Agreement 'would not have acknowledged the legitimacy of the aspirations of many Irish people for a united Ireland. And without that acknowledgement we would have no peace process'. That was seen then as absurd: a wrong-headed reading of history and a morally perverse way to achieve that specific end. But this has now become a 'post-truth' political fact.

One of the most disturbing effects of the 2017 General Election is that the slovenly sociability between sentimentality and badness is now at the heart of a potential party of UK government. The appalling subtext is this: slovenly, virtue signalling, sentimentality fellow travels with badness and the post-truth 'fact' for many young people is: 'to make an omelette it is necessary to break a few eggs'. To which George Orwell's response to such Newspeak is appropriate: 'Yes, but where's the omelette?' Where indeed? This is exactly the world view Hegel raged against in his own time.

Third is the exclusion of the majority. The Haass Report confidently proclaimed: 'What happened in the past cannot be changed'. The concern which many people have – and not just unionists - is that what is happening is exactly the past changing. In one of the best books on the mentality of IRA terrorism, *The IRA and Armed Struggle*, the Spanish academic Rogelio Alonso had an intimation that slovenly sociability between sentimentality and badness would write the majority out of history. 'What place', he asked, 'will be occupied in history by those who, with immense civic and human virtue, have resisted using violence, in spite of having the same grievances as those who resorted to terror?'

He thought it essential to delegitimise both republican and loyalist violence. This was the virtuous task of the times for it 'is a debt contracted by history'. Implicit too is the view that, unless the historical debt is properly discharged, the past could well repeat itself. That was also the conclusion of Douglas Murray's book *Bloody Sunday: Truth, Lies and the Saville Inquiry*.

Unfortunately, 'the past' now seems to be understood only as a dialogue between armed republicanism (sentimentally glossed) and the British state (which colluded against rights, virtue, law and justice).

Henry Patterson once argued that the book *Lost Lives* is sufficient testimony against such a comprehensive re-writing of history. Can we be so sure any longer? For all their moral self-righteousness, some in Alliance now seem to have succumbed to 'slovenly sentimentality'. Equally, some others in the SDLP don't seem to mind that even John Hume is being written out of history. All that is necessary for slovenly sentimentality to triumph is the dissemination of something more allusive and ill-defined than simple justification of terror. It is, rather, the explicit use (or avoidance) of certain words - in the idea of human tragedy rather than human agency; in the power of suggestion rather than interrogation, intimating state collusion. One example reveals the collusion of the slovenly (journalism in this case) and the bad.

When the Radio 4 Today Programme covered the Report of the Smithwick Tribunal, the BBC's Northern Ireland correspondent presented a summary of the findings on the murder of Superintendents Breen and Buchanan. James Naughtie interjected: '*All part of the Dirty War, of course*' to which the reporter responded: '*Yes*'. That exchange represents unreflective collusion and all the more dangerous for its historical implications. The Dirty War thesis assumes that 'one side was as bad as the other', that one shouldn't make ethical judgements and everyone knows how it was – even the 'dogs in the street'.

There is no necessary intent to deceive, merely the seduction of the assumed 'pattern' or 'theme' in history which stands in for serious historical understanding. However innocent or inadvertent that example may seem, it implies a narrative about Northern Ireland's history suggesting equivalence and justification – equivalence between the acts of terrorists and security forces, justification for the IRA's campaign.

Fifth, is institutional inversion. That it is the BBC – especially BBC NI - which disseminates that sort of narrative feeds widespread public disquiet about the role of institutions and their effect. It feeds a pervasive sense that institutional structures (from BBC to courts) are delivering for terrorists and not for victims;

or, to put that otherwise, that institutional priorities have become unethically skewed by slovenly sentimentality in favour of the bad and against the good. It has affected universities too, and not just in Northern Ireland, especially when it comes to 'terrorism studies'. It has been well-exposed by the work of David Jones and MLR Smith

They argue that this type of academic work simply exploits *the relativist turn in Western thought given to them by a Western tradition of self-questioning in order to equate liberalâ€"democratic pluralism with the worst kinds of oppressive tyranny.* Jones and Smith think that there is a curiously incoherent empathy with the motives of those engaged in terrorism, promoting moral confusion (though in Northern Ireland it is possibly not so curious). In short: *In the looking glass world of critical terror studies reveals that we are all terrorists now and must empathize with those sub-state actors who have recourse to violence for whatever motive.*

Where we end up is here: *terrorists are really no different from us. In fact, there is terror as the weapon of the weak and the far worse and coercive terror of the liberal state.*

Indeed, it is exactly where we have ended up in Northern Ireland. One of the objectives of terrorism during the Troubles was to alienate nationalist opinion from public institutions. The post-Troubles objective is to alienate Middle Ulster from public institutions with the assistance of the slovenly sentimentality of many of those same institutions.

What can be done?

The argument is that on so-called 'legacy' issues there exists a tendentious agenda, advanced under the guise of a humanitarian concern, one which extols histrionically notions like 'justice' and 'emancipation'. Needless to say, it's mainly about power (and the exclusion of those who disagree): power in the sense of controlling the political agenda and power also in the sense of controlling the language, thereby imposing – somewhat ironically – an entirely uncritical intellectual orthodoxy.

It is essential to mobilise against and confront this slovenly sociability between sentimentality and badness. It needs to be challenged consistently, coherently and intelligently.

It requires an active civil society engagement – to re-occupy the public realm - and not just a party political response. It requires changing the language of public discourse. It will be uncomfortable and difficult. But it is essential.

Do Nationalists and Unionists have different conceptions of what are human rights?

Human Rights Consortium Festival

Queen's University Belfast School of Law

Moot Court, Monday 11 December 2017

Councillor Jeffrey Dudgeon MBE with Declan Kearney MLA of Sinn Fein and Sophie Long of the Green Party/PUP. Introduction by Professor Brice Dickson former NIHRC Chief Commissioner

Human rights are a post-war concept, best exemplified by the European Convention on Human Rights (ECHR).

Predating that is a line of connection back to the 1689 Bill of Rights and, obliquely, a century later the 1789 US Bill of Rights.

Civil and religious liberty for all is their watchword, being a central tenet for all Unionists and Protestants not just for those in the Loyal Orders. And that belief is grounded in <u>individual</u> conscience.

The contemporary approach is best exemplified by the Preamble to the European Convention on Human Rights. Often ignored, it proclaims that "Fundamental rights and freedoms are best maintained by an effective political democracy and a common understanding and observance of human rights."

Certainly maintaining an "effective political democracy" is the core component of our fundamental rights and freedoms. More human rights must not be allowed to replace or erode that.

This creates a significant point of distinction between Unionists and nationalists or separatists (and their radical allies). We cannot have politics done through human rights. That is elitism and the road back to autocracy.

The line will be fine – but significant social and economic rights are too far over the line, something I will come to later when I address the Northern Ireland Bill of Rights notion that is so close to the minds of many in this room.

Am I a human right activist? When so described, I know it sounds wrong because I am a Unionist. I may let myself be described as such to annoy some people, but I am much more than that. Anyway Unionists are perceived as against human rights. I recognise that to the extent I have even unconsciously absorbed the perception!

Our "effective political democracy" is currently Westminster and local councils – the latter which are still shorn of normal local government powers like education, culture and health even parking. In Belfast where I am a councillor, we got planning powers back in 2015 but so much more should have been returned. We were then denied the promised regeneration powers in a Stormont stitch-up. Local government and councils, I can tell you, work.

Pointlessly, Sinn Fein boycott Westminster, as they once did the Dail. With the elimination of the SDLP and the UUP from the House of Commons we have only the DUP there. No Irish nationalists. But that is not the DUP's fault.

I was reminded of the power and force of Westminster by Seamus Mallon last Friday at Notting Hill – the DFA consulate in Belfast – when at a book launch he spoke fondly of his memories of 20 years of political action in the House of Commons. To my mind, Westminster is a living market place where MPs come to trade. The Stormont mausoleum has never been that, nor will it ever be.

There is a core background reason that marks Unionists and their attitudes out as distinct, something not respected by nationalists nor accepted by those Protestants of a progressive outlook who decry the strong conservatism in that community dominant since the 1880s. Unionism is about protecting the status quo and has been for a century. It is a movement with a single aim and purpose. It would be better if it did not do politics but since partition and the imposition of Stormont it was obliged by London to concentrate only on the very thing that divide us.

Without the broader involvement of the main British political parties, as was apparent and valuable in the 19th century in the north, we have been fated to live out a perpetual ethnic conflict.

Unionism has to be defensive. It can only lose once and is therefore understandably obdurate and intransigent. Not nice to look at, which is why I try to do it with a smile, and by giving respect to opponents. But we don't have a single friend in the radical, leftist, international community, unlike Irish nationalism. That leads to having differing outlooks and responses. It is an experience increasingly shared by the United States, and obviously Israel, and will have increasing consequences.

It inevitably makes Unionism intrinsically conservative not progressive except in a small number of individual cases like Montgomery Hyde, MP for North Belfast from 1950 to 1959, and a rare advocate in the Commons in the 1950s for homosexual law reform and an end to capital punishment. My hero.

So-called liberal Protestants who are easily influenced by the cries of nationalism peel off in every generation and are lost or emigrate.

A huge factor in the apparent difference between Unionists and Republicans on rights is the failure of the human rights community in its broadest sense to address paramilitary violence.

The community has eschewed the use of international agreements and consortia to undermine paramilitarism. The failure to write about it, research or campaign about it, is a stain on its reputation.

There has been and will be no greater denial of human rights in our lifetime than the 3,700 in this small area, not to mention the countless injuries and the destruction of property on a vast scale.

The anniversary of the murder of Edgar Graham was only last week. He was shot yards from where we are sitting. Like myself, he was an elected representative for the UUP in South Belfast, and also a law lecturer at this university. His murderers have never been arraigned, nor will they be. His death has been the subject of no inquiries, resolutions or protests. An editorial in the News Letter on Friday was the only public mention. The same applies to the assassination of the South Belfast MP, Robert Bradford (and the caretaker at the Finaghy community centre). Both killings were contrary to the spirit of the ECHR and of course the letter.

Does Article 2's 'Right to Life' only apply to the 10% killed by the state, lawfully, in most instances? This is worth pursuing in academic circles.

I example most recently the academy's silence over the OTR letters issue but there are so many more.

Pro-union (for want of a better phrase) cases at the Strasbourg court can be counted on the fingers of one hand. Indeed only one comes to mind – an early 1980s Article 2 right to life case concerning the sectarian murder of UDR soldiers on the border. It fell at the first hurdle.

At that time, the concept of non-state actors like the IRA being held culpable at Strasbourg (or through the work of Amnesty) had not got off the ground. It has a little since and should – by use of the ingenuity we are familiar with in modern jurisprudence, be advanced a great deal more.

In extenso, ECHR's Article 2 interestingly reads:

1. Everyone's right to life shall be protected by law. No one shall be deprived of his life intentionally save in the execution of a sentence of a court following his conviction of a crime for which this penalty is provided by law.

2. Deprivation of life shall not be regarded as inflicted in contravention of this article when it results from the use of force which is no more than absolutely necessary:

a   in defence of any person from unlawful violence;

b. in order to effect a lawful arrest or to prevent escape of a person lawfully detained;

c. in action lawfully taken for the purpose of quelling a riot or insurrection.

It is the unbalanced Strasbourg interpretation of this Article on which the Legacy industry bases its ceaseless demands for more inquests to be reopened.

As I tell people, law is not about truth, justice or fair play. It is rare that any of these can actually be achieved in the elaboration of the legal system.

Law is essentially about stability and civil peace, about a system of civilisation and a structure of independent courts that enable people who have nothing in common, or indeed conflicting interests, to accept living together – without resort to violence. That measure is then normally reserved to the state. However we went through some forty years of war where peace was not the case. Law and human rights almost died.

There is also a costs imbalance involving the use or misuse of legal aid which should be addressed, perhaps by this university. It makes unionist human rights case infrequent.

I have difficulties with what is called 'the equality agenda'. I believe in equal opportunity. Also in diversity. However when it comes to a conflict between human rights and equality, human rights should be allowed to trump equality. Not the other way round.

The balance is heading in the wrong direction, especially as the concept of equality is now inextricably the agenda of one party.

I turn now to the Bill of Rights which never materialised. Some will know I played a role in the Bill of Rights Forum, another NIO talking shop that led nowhere.

On that occasion the UUP, DUP, and Alliance Parties were united in their rejection of the attempt, alongside that of the NIHRC, to bring about 'An All Singing All Dancing' Bill of Rights.

To set the record straight, there was no commitment to legislating any Bill of Rights in the Belfast Agreement nor indeed did the particular circumstances mentioned mean anything more than adding a few local aspects e.g. on parades – had a Bill come to pass.

The agreement did provide for the Northern Ireland Human Rights Commission (NIHRC) to give advice to the Secretary of State on:

'The scope for defining in Westminster legislation rights supplementing the ECHR reflecting the particular circumstances of Northern Ireland and reflecting the principles of mutual respect and parity of esteem.'

But NIHRC took, in my view, a misguided and quite unduly expansionist view of this very specific brief.

Finally, it tendered the required advice and the advice was rejected by government. And that ended the matter. Deceptively twisting the remit or pretending there was a promise to enact a Bill in the Good Friday Agreement only angers Unionists. The ECHR remains in place as a hugely effective safeguard for us all but its rulings are not divine and can go awry.

NIHRC caused a fissure with the Unionist community over this, and if the human rights community seeks further expansion as a result of the Stormont House Agreement that will cause yet more resentment in the community.

Did Unionist (or liberal voices dissenting from the prevailing NIHRC ideology) receive any, or any fair, participation in university seminars and conferences? Of course not.

The Bill of Rights issue exemplified the overplaying of a hand which helped bring rights into disrepute.

NIHRC has been a disaster in its first three manifestations although the 4th seems an improvement, reverting to key 1960s matters where we were left out of reform.

Would that it now took up those issues that so frighten the Equality Commission and are a legacy of London pandering to the Catholic Church, which was always allowed a bye-ball by the Northern Ireland Office and London.

I instance the exception for all teacher appointments in our fair employment laws and the failure to extend the 1998 Northern Ireland Act's Section 75 sexual orientation protection to schools. Sinn Fein – you will recall – used the much-hated Petition of Concern to block the reform of the teacher exception law. These issues have no traction amongst the bien pensants in Belfast.

Unionists have been too polite, and nervous of appearing sectarian to address them forcefully while abortion is the key issue for the next decade. Back to the 1960s again.

My final point is that the Unionist view seems never to receive academic articulation: Were there any 'Unionist' human rights academic lawyers ready to challenge the expansionist views of, for instance, the NI Human Rights Commission?

Is it possible for someone outside of the current conventional wisdom to get a job at QUB or UU? Could a Unionist activist let alone a DUP member work in one of the law departments?

Don't be silly, it is impossible. There is no chill factor in operation. It is a freeze factor.

There is a monoculture especially in Legacy matters and a complete reversal of the previous situation where our law schools were timid and unadventurous.

In conclusion, one area where I would like to see you use your experience and knowledge is in relation to human rights in wartime. We have now reached the position where the state and its agencies are incapable of using hard and effective methods internally yet they and the military are given an almost free hand abroad. Even with self-imposed restraints, casualties and destruction abound. That balance needs reset. It might mean fewer rights (and their enforcement) locally but a greater and necessary trammelling of military actions.

(An abbreviated version of Jeff Dudgeon's talk was published in *The News Letter* on 29 December 2017.)

Extracts from the Stormont House Agreement etc.

The Stormont House Agreement (December 2014); The Fresh Start Agreement (November 2015); The Independent Commission on Information Retrieval (January 2016); The Stormont House Agreement (Legacy) Bill (n.d.)

Editorial Note on Legacy Documentation

The Stormont House Agreement (SHA)

It is described by UK Government Publications (www.gov.uk/government/publications/the-stormont-house-agreement),   as an "agreement reached with Northern Ireland's political leaders" after 11 weeks of talks at Stormont. (In fact, the Ulster Unionist Party, although a participant in the talks, withheld its agreement.) The Agreement was published on 23 December 2014.

The provisions dealing with 'The Past' in paragraphs 21 to 55 of the SHA are below.

The SHA also altered the structure of the Northern Ireland institutions. The number of representatives in the Northern Ireland Assembly was agreed to be reduced, from six MLAs per Westminster constituency to five in time for the 2021 Assembly election. However this was actually implemented in May 2017 due to the calling of an early election. It also envisaged reforms being put in place to allow parties to decline from joining the Northern Ireland Executive, and instead receive funding as an official opposition. By the 2016 election the number of Stormont departments were also reduced from twelve to nine.

The Fresh Start Agreement

This was published on 17 November 2015. It is entitled 'The Stormont Agreement and Implementation Plan'. A strap line on the face of the document declares: "An agreement to consolidate the peace, secure stability, enable progress and offer hope."

It contains a Ministerial introduction signed by the First Minister (then Peter Robinson MLA) and the deputy First Minister (then Martin McGuinness MLA) and forewords from the Secretary of State for Northern Ireland (then Theresa Villiers MP) and the Irish Minister of Foreign Affairs and Trade (then Charles Flanagan TD).

It was preceded by 10 weeks of discussions involving the two governments and the five main Northern Ireland parties entitled to participate in the Executive.

The main focus of the Agreement was on addressing "the legacy and impact of paramilitary activity", on the necessary financial reforms and on "Welfare and Tax Credits Top-Ups".

It was also an implementation review of the Stormont House Agreement. Below are the (few) legacy related provisions.

The Independent Commission on Information Retrieval (ICIR)

Paragraphs 41 to 50 of the SHA provide for the ICIR. On 21 January 2016 the Secretary of State announced in the House of Commons that the two governments had signed an international agreement "to enable the establishment of the ICIR and set out its functions". However, the treaty has not yet been published because the Secretary of State proposes to do this only when the legislation on the other bodies is being debated in Parliament. Below is the text of her statement which gives some (limited) information.

Stormont House Agreement Legacy Bill – Proposed Bodies

It appears that a draft Bill has been prepared to establish the various bodies proposed by the SHA. A draft text was released to the parties involved in the recent talks but no version has been made publicly available.

It is understood that the Northern Ireland Office intends to release a consultation paper on 'implementation' but this appears to await agreement by the two main parties. Presumably, the consultation paper will include a copy of the text of the draft Bill.

Text of paragraphs 21 to 55 of the Stormont House Agreement: The Past

The participants agree:

21. As part of the transition to long-term peace and stability the participants agree that an approach to dealing with the past is necessary which respects the following principles:

- promoting reconciliation;

- upholding the rule of law;

- acknowledging and addressing the suffering of victims and survivors;

- facilitating the pursuit of justice and information recovery;

- is human rights compliant; and

- is balanced, proportionate, transparent, fair and equitable.

Consistent with those principles, the participants have agreed as follows:

22. The Executive will, by 2016, establish an *Oral History Archive* to provide a central place for people from all backgrounds (and from throughout the UK and Ireland) to share experiences and narratives related to the Troubles. As well as collecting new material, this archive will attempt to draw together and work with existing oral history projects.

23. The sharing of experiences will be entirely voluntary and consideration will be given to protecting contributors, and the body itself, from defamation claims. The Archive will bring forward proposals on the circumstances and timing of contributions being made public.

24. The Archive will be independent and free from political interference.

25. A research project will be established as part of the Archive, led by academics to produce a factual historical timeline and statistical analysis of the Troubles, to report within 12 months.

26. The Executive will take steps to ensure that *Victims and Survivors* have access to high quality services, respecting the principles of choice and need. The needs of victims who do not live in Northern Ireland should also be recognised.

27. The Commission for Victims and Survivors' recommendation for a comprehensive Mental Trauma Service will be implemented. This will operate within the NHS but will work closely with the Victims and Survivors Service (VSS), and other organisations and groups who work directly with victims and survivors.

28. Further work will be undertaken to seek an acceptable way forward on the proposal for a pension for severely physically injured victims in Northern Ireland.

29. Victims and survivors will be given access to advocate-counsellor assistance if they wish.

Historical Investigations Unit

30. Legislation will establish a new independent body to take forward investigations into outstanding Troubles-related deaths; the Historical Investigations Unit (HIU). The body will take forward outstanding cases from the HET process, and the legacy work of the Police Ombudsman for Northern Ireland (PONI). A report will be produced in each case.

31. Processes dealing with the past should be victim-centred. Legacy inquests will continue as a separate process to the HIU. Recent domestic and European judgments have demonstrated that the legacy inquest process is not providing access to a sufficiently effective investigation within an acceptable timeframe. In light of this, the Executive will take appropriate steps to improve the way the legacy inquest function is conducted to comply with ECHR Article 2 requirements.

32. Appropriate governance arrangements will be put in place to ensure the operational independence of the two different elements of the work of the HIU.

33. The HIU will have dedicated family support staff who will involve the next of kin from the beginning and provide them with expert advice and other necessary support throughout the process.

34. The HIU will consider all cases in respect of which HET and PONI have not completed their work, including HET cases which have already been identified as requiring re-examination. Families may apply to have other

cases considered for criminal investigation by the HIU if there is new evidence, which was not previously before the HET, which is relevant to the identification and eventual prosecution of the perpetrator.

35. As with existing criminal investigations, the decision to prosecute is a matter for the DPP and the HIU may consult his office on evidentiary issues in advance of submitting a file.

36. When cases are transferred from HET and PONI, all relevant case files held by those existing bodies will be passed to the new body. In respect of its criminal investigations, the HIU will have full policing powers. In respect of the cases from PONI, the HIU will have equivalent powers to that body.

37. The UK Government makes clear that it will make full disclosure to the HIU. In order to ensure that no individuals are put at risk, and that the Government's duty to keep people safe and secure is upheld, Westminster legislation will provide for equivalent measures to those that currently apply to existing bodies so as to prevent any damaging onward disclosure of information by the HIU.

38. HIU will be overseen by the Northern Ireland Policing Board.

39. The necessary arrangements will be put in place to ensure the HIU has the full co-operation of all relevant Irish authorities, including disclosure of information and documentation. This will include arrangements for cooperation between criminal investigation agencies in both jurisdictions and arrangements for obtaining evidence for use in court proceedings. Where additional legislation is required, it will be brought forward by the Irish Government.

40.   In order to ensure expeditious investigations, the HIU should aim to complete its work within five years of its establishment.

Independent Commission on Information Retrieval (ICIR)

41.   A new body, which will respect the sovereign integrity of each jurisdiction, will be established by the UK and Irish Governments, called the Independent Commission on Information Retrieval (ICIR), building on the precedent provided by the Independent Commission on the Location of Victims' Remains. The objective of the ICIR will be to enable victims and survivors to seek and privately receive information about the (Troubles-related) deaths of their next of kin.

42.   Individuals from both the UK and Ireland will be able to seek information from the ICIR.

43.   Once established, the body will run for no longer than 5 years.

44.   The ICIR will be led by five members: an independent chairperson who may be of international standing and will be appointed by the UK and Irish Governments, in consultation with OFMDFM, together with two nominees appointed by the First and deputy First Minister, one each appointed by the UK Government and the Irish Government.

45.   The ICIR's remit will cover both jurisdictions and will have the same functions in each. It will be entirely separate from the justice system. The ICIR will also be free to seek information from other jurisdictions, and both governments undertake to support such requests.

46. The ICIR will not disclose information provided to it to law enforcement or intelligence agencies and this information will be inadmissible in criminal and civil proceedings. These facts will be made clear to those seeking to access information through the body.

47. The ICIR will be given the immunities and privileges of an international body and would not be subject to judicial review, Freedom of Information, Data Protection and National Archives legislation, in either jurisdiction.

48. Legislation will be taken forward by the UK Government, the Irish Government and the Assembly to implement the above decision on inadmissibility.

49. The ICIR will not disclose the identities of people who provide information. No individual who provides information to the body will be immune from prosecution for any crime committed should the required evidential test be satisfied by other means.

50. The ICIR will be held accountable to the principles of independence, rigour, fairness and balance, transparency and proportionality.

Implementation and Reconciliation

51. An Implementation and Reconciliation Group (IRG) will be established to oversee themes, archives and information recovery. After 5 years a report on themes will be commissioned by the IRG from independent academic experts. Any potential evidence base for patterns and themes should be referred to the IRG from any of the legacy mechanisms, who may comment on the level of co-operation received, for the IRG's analysis and assessment. This process should be conducted with sensitivity and rigorous

intellectual integrity, devoid of any political interference.

52. Promoting reconciliation will underlie all of the work of the IRG. It will encourage and support other initiatives that contribute to reconciliation, better understanding of the past and reducing sectarianism.

53. In the context of the work of the IRG, the UK and Irish Governments will consider statements of acknowledgement and would expect others to do the same.

54. The Body will be eleven strong. Publicly elected representatives will not be eligible for appointment. The chair shall be a person of independent and international standing and will be nominated by the First Minister and deputy First Minister. The other appointments will be nominated as follows: DUP - 3 nominees, Sinn Fein – 2 nominees, SDLP – 1 nominee, UUP – 1 nominee, and Alliance Party – 1 nominee and one nominee each from the UK and Irish Governments.

55. The UK and Irish Governments recognise that there are outstanding investigations and allegations into Troubles-related incidents, including a number of cross-border incidents. They commit to co-operation with all bodies involved to enable their effective operation, recognising their distinctive functions, and to bring forward legislation where necessary.

The Fresh Start Agreement Provisions

In her foreword to the document the Secretary of State included the following reference to the legacy institutions: "Despite some significant progress we were not able at this stage to reach a final agreement on the establishment of new bodies to deal with the past. The Government continues to support these provisions of the Stormont House Agreement and to providing better outcomes for victims and survivors. We will now reflect with the other participants on how we can move forward and achieve broad consensus for legislation."

In Section 'D' (UK Government Financial Support), paragraph 7.2 states that the Government 'will provide a number of further flexibilities' including that: "any underspend on new legacy funding in 2015-16 may be carried forward to 2020-21 (but funding for bodies to deal with the past is subject to agreement on their establishment)."

Section 'F' (Implementation of the Stormont House Agreement) states in regard to 'The Past': "The parties to this Agreement reaffirm their commitment to the full and fair implementation of the SHA provisions on the past.

A large measure of agreement has been found on the detail of many of the issues addressed by the SHA. Some of these remain a work in progress.

While progress has been made on most aspects of the legacy of the past, we have been unable to agree a way forward on some of the key issues.

There remains a need to resolve the outstanding issues and the UK Government and Irish Government will reflect on the options for a process to enable this."

The Independent Commission on Information Retrieval

Statement in Parliament given by the Secretary of State on 21 January 2016

The cross-party talks that ran from 8 September to 17 November last year, which culminated in the Fresh Start agreement, brought us closer than ever before to consensus on the best way to deal with Northern Ireland's past. While we established much common ground, it was not possible to reach agreement on all issues. I am committed to working with the Northern Ireland parties, with the Irish Government as appropriate, and with representatives of victims and survivors, to build on the progress made during the talks. The UK Government is determined to resolve the outstanding issues that are preventing the establishment of the legacy institutions set out in the Stormont House Agreement.

One of these institutions is the Independent Commission on Information Retrieval (ICIR). This will be an independent body designed to enable victims and survivors privately to receive information about the Troubles-related deaths of their next of kin. As set out in the Stormont House Agreement, and building on the precedent of the Independent Commission on the Location of Victims' Remains, the ICIR will be an international body. To that end, the UK and Irish Governments have signed an international agreement to enable the establishment of the ICIR and to set out its functions. Today I have placed a copy of this treaty in the libraries of both Houses.

The ICIR will be an important institution which will help victims and survivors to seek information which it has not been possible to obtain by other means. Engagement by families with the ICIR will be entirely voluntary. Information provided to the ICIR about deaths within its remit will not be admissible in court, something which families will always be told in advance. The ICIR will not, however, provide any form of amnesty or immunity from prosecution. This Government believes in the rule of law and would not countenance such a step. As the Stormont House Agreement set out, information provided to the ICIR will be protected but no individual will be protected from prosecution if evidence is obtained by other means. It is the Government's intention that the legislation needed to implement the ICIR will contain provisions clearly setting this out.

It had been our aim to lay the treaty before Parliament at the same time as introducing the legislation required to establish the legacy bodies. However, as agreement has not yet been reached on this legislation, this is not possible. Once any treaty is formally laid, Parliament has a period of 21 sitting days, in which it can resolve that the treaty should not be ratified, in accordance with the Constitutional Reform and Governance Act 2010. I believe that it would be best if this consideration took place alongside the legislation, which will contain more detail about how the ICIR will function. I propose therefore formally to lay the treaty once we are able also to introduce legislation. These particular circumstances mean that placing a copy of the treaty in the libraries of both Houses is an appropriate way to ensure that Parliament is aware of the text of the treaty, without instigating the formal process of consideration.

In addition to the ICIR, the Stormont House Agreement envisaged the establishment of the Historical Investigations Unit, the Oral History Archive and the Implementation and Reconciliation Group. Together, this set of institutions provides the best opportunity to help Northern Ireland deal with its past and provide better outcomes for victims and survivors, the people who we must never forget suffered more than anyone else as a result of the Troubles. The Government is committed to implementing the Stormont House Agreement and to establishing the legacy bodies it contains. I will continue to meet victims' representatives and others over the coming days and weeks to discuss these matters and to build support for the new institutions.

CPSIA information can be obtained
at www.ICGtesting.com
Printed in the USA
LVHW05s1419161018
593795LV00001B/93/P